The Quirky Medium

The Quirky Medium

The extraordinary life of an unlikely
clairvoyant, star of TV's *Rescue Mediums*

Alison Wynne-Ryder

A record of this publication is available from the British Library.

ISBN 978-1-907203-47-3

Typesetting by Wordzworth Ltd
www.wordzworth.com

Cover design by Titanium Design Ltd
www.titaniumdesign.co.uk

Cover photograph by the author, portrait by Carol Ryder

Published by Local Legend
www.local-legend.co.uk

**LOCAL
LEGEND**

Dedication

To John, whose mantra (particularly when we feel lost!) is "All paths lead to somewhere." I couldn't have done any of this without your love, support and endless proof reading.

Also to Olivia, Madeleine, Alexandra and Jason, my gorgeous grand-children who have lit up my life in a way I could never have imagined, and to Lauren, my daughter, who tells me like it is and helps to keep my feet on the ground when my head is in the clouds!

Acknowledgements

For their input, support and assistance whilst writing this book, I thank my mum Joyce for always believing in me and a big thank you also to my sister Carol for helping me with the presentation of the book. I am also grateful to Nigel Peace of Local Legend for all his encouragement and advice.

Special thanks to John and Lauren Garnett-Mackie who helped to edit my manuscript, to those of you who were kind enough to share your spiritual stories with me, and to all my friends who have stuck by me through the laughter and the tears. A thank you from the bottom of my heart goes to my loved ones in the spirit world, especially my Grandma who told me that I would write the book.

I thank my spirit guides Zamil, Ruby, Star and my tall and wise First Nations guide, known simply as The Wise One. I would also like to thank Amy, a little spirit girl who comes forward to help, particularly when I am working with children. And last, but certainly not least, thank you to the angels for absolutely everything.

About the Author

Alison Wynne-Ryder is a clairvoyant medium of international fame, working with spirit in order to bring comfort and guidance to her many clients worldwide.

She is an 'Angel Lady with a difference', helping others to bring the love of angels into their home so that they can release old patterns in their personal lives. Alison is also co-host of the TV show *Rescue Mediums*, bringing new peace for homeowners and sending misguided spirits 'to the light', as well as hosting and guesting on many radio blogs and stations.

She still finds time somehow to practise as a Reiki Master and to write features for spiritual magazines such as *The Magical Times* and *Prediction*, and her work has been featured in the national press.

Alison lives in Cheshire with her husband John, her dog Libby and cats Tara and Celeste.

http://www.spiritualit.net/
Follow Alison on Twitter: *@rescuemediumali*

Contents

Introduction

"Go confidently in the direction of your dreams. Live the life you have imagined."

—Henry David Thoreau

When I receive messages from the spirit world I never ignore them! So when my lovely Grandma came forward in a meditation last year and told me I would be writing a book about my memoirs and spirituality, I had to sit up and take notice. As I started to write, I received a clear message from spirit: "Don't worry - just write the book and we will show you the way."

This book has been written for a number of reasons. Whenever I give talks or take part in interviews, people ask me how I knew I was psychic, how I became a medium and how they too can live a spiritual life. I am also asked what it's like being part of a psychic TV show, so I have included first-hand accounts of working on *Rescue Mediums* (filmed in Canada and airing on W Network, OWN and in the UK on CBS Reality and in other countries around the world).

I have included emails about my experiences as well as extracts from my spiritual journal which include others' true stories. There are many amazing accounts of angels and the paranormal. These include the vivid clairvoyant visions experienced by a very special and gifted little girl, and the story of a beautiful young woman who for years has received very strange messages and signs from the spirit world about the characters from a well-known children's story! These signs have now become so strong that she cannot ignore them; my research into the irrefutable evidence she presents leads me to believe that her spirit guide is someone very special… read her story and decide for yourself!

Indeed, you may believe that you also have psychic abilities. If so, or you just want to know more about spirituality in general, then this book is for you! For those new to the subject I have included a chapter entitled the ABC of Spirituality which briefly covers the esoteric from angels right through to Zen and everything in between.

Be assured that each and every one of you deserves the good things in life and, although the demands of our modern world can undoubtedly be stressful, by the time you turn the last page in the book you will feel so enlightened and spiritually aware you will want to share your spiritual experiences with others.

In telling my story I promise that I will not try to force my beliefs or experiences onto you. This is my own personal spiritual journey; no doubt yours will be different. Nor will I pretend that I am in any way special, that my psychic abilities are in any way hereditary and handed down from a family of clairvoyants who read crystal balls and tea leaves. What I will do is share my story with you, warts and all, about how my psychic abilities blossomed and grew into something very special. In doing so I hope to help you overcome your fears and learn how to live in the present moment, enjoying what life has to offer. You are in charge of your own life and once you realise this, and understand the magic of your soul, you will have the courage to step onto your own spiritual path with confidence and ease.

If I can do it, so can you!

CHAPTER 1

Ending and Beginning

"Fear has a large shadow, but he himself is small."

—RUTH GENDLER

Of all the people that would eventually become a clairvoyant medium, I am probably one of the most unlikely. I was always frightened of death and ghosts! But let me share some 'shivers down the spine' moments of my life.

At nine years old I remember playing in my bedroom when I heard the door open. I thought it was my Mum coming in to check on me but to my horror there was nobody present. As I watched, the door proceeded to close by itself and emitted an eerie, violent scraping sound similar to that of someone dragging their nails down a blackboard. I was completely frozen and paralysed with fear. My ears rang with a loud heart-rending scream that echoed throughout the entire room. A few moments later as I sat in shock, I realised that the scream had in fact emanated from me and had bolted out from the very bottom of my lungs… Adrenaline coursed through my body and I knew that I had to get out of there fast. The next thing I remember was hurtling down the stairs at breakneck speed, crashing into my Mum who had come to investigate the commotion. She looked petrified but she certainly didn't let on. Once she'd managed to calm me down, she marched me up the stairs into the bedroom and opened the door.

"There," she said, "it's just that the door needs oiling and there is nothing to worry about. There is always a normal explanation for everything." I preferred my Mum's interpretation of events because the alternative didn't bear thinking about. Little did I know that there was far more to come. Far, far more.

Not long after that I was lying in bed and desperately trying to get to sleep. It was pitch black in the room and I had an awful feeling that I was not alone. However, as tiredness took over I started to drift off to sleep. In the darkness, in my semi-conscious state, I felt the bedclothes moving. I tried to convince myself that it was my Mum tucking me in; however, deep down I knew I hadn't heard her enter the room. I meekly called out "Goodnight" to her, hoping against hope to hear her voice but when only silence answered, with horror I realised it wasn't Mum in the room with me at all, but someone who was not of this world. The bedclothes moved again, I tried to shout out for Mum but no words came out of my mouth. My limbs felt heavy and I realised I couldn't move any part of my body – I was literally petrified.

It was at this point that I was greeted with a vision of a lion in a cage, and as I started to concentrate on the lion the scary feelings went away, along with my 'visitor'. Each time I was plagued with visitors after that, the lion would appear. Looking back over my childhood, I realise now that it was my spirit guide giving me the image for protection and strength. To this day I don't know who came into my room that night, but it was the start of many similar experiences for me. I certainly couldn't put it down to imagination, and this was only the very beginning.

Jackie had gone quiet so I knew there was something badly wrong! She was staring ahead, her eyes glazed and she was making an awful growling noise which made the hairs on the back of my neck stand up. I knew at that point that no matter how much I called to her she wouldn't hear me as 'he' had taken her over. I waited for him to communicate but, when it came, it made me jump and threw me off balance. I have never been so scared in all my life. Why was I doing this, what do I do now? Jackie was flailing her arms around in the air as he made her shout, "Hang the bastards, hang the bastards!" My heart was beating so loudly I was sure the sound would be picked up by the camera guys and I thought, "Oh God, please help, how on Earth am I going to get this one over?" And so it begins....

"Begin at the beginning, and go on 'til you come to the end: then stop."

—LEWIS CARROLL, ALICE IN WONDERLAND

As a child I was totally alone with a gift that I didn't understand, and I certainly didn't see it as a gift because I assumed that everyone experienced the same. However, I learned very early on that this was not the case, which meant in the end I had no-one I could talk to or go to for answers. In school I was referred to as 'Alice in Wonderland' by teachers and pupils alike and would often drift off into my own imaginary world as I preferred it there. I had one sister, Carol, and we had strict parents.

I used to sleep walk a lot and talk in my sleep (when I eventually got to sleep, that is). All in all I was an odd child but I didn't know why. We lived in a terraced house in an industrial town called Runcorn in the north-west of England. I attended the local primary, junior and secondary schools. There is a saying that your school years are the best years of your life; I disagree – I hated school and couldn't wait to leave. I could never understand the conflict and gossip that went on at my secondary school and I always felt on a completely different wavelength to everyone else. It was hard to come to terms with my gift as a teenager and I am sure that as you are reading this it will resonate with many of you 'old souls' who have been through similar experiences yourself.

I have always adored books and as a child I forever had my head buried in one. I often felt that I could jump into one of the pages and escape from reality. My favourite author when I was growing up was Enid Blyton. I loved her stories of the Enchanted Wood and the Magic Faraway Tree. I adored how magical everything was and I imagined myself as one of the children visiting each wonderful land at the top of the tree, my favourites being the 'Land of do as you please' and the 'Land of spells'. I wonder why that was?

In times of turmoil and darkness, I always knew there was something else out there looking after me and I strove to find out what it was. I can only describe what I felt as a deep inner 'knowing' that I would always be looked after, but I didn't know who by. The feeling was so strong I didn't dare question its authenticity because although I didn't have tangible proof that another realm existed apart from the Earth, I just knew and totally believed in my heart that it did.

I spent a lot of time with my cousin Gillian when I was growing up. We were the same age (three months apart) and we had a 'secret den' at our Grandma's house. It was her old shed, but we thought it was the bees' knees! We asked my Uncle Arthur, Gillian's father, to paint the walls of the secret den in psychedelic colours and we used to make up adventures and our own fantasy lands that we would 'visit'. We had carpet picnics and pretended that we were on a secret mission or on surveillance. We hid every time we heard footsteps, thinking that spies were coming to get us! We even made up our own courtroom drama with our own characters and I enjoyed shouting "Guilty as charged!" It made sense that later in life I ended up working for the police for thirteen years, liaising with the CPS and the courts, and marrying a police sergeant – to say nothing of my psychic investigative work on the show Rescue Mediums.

It's funny but, as a child, anything is possible and you make your own entertainment. It's only when you get older and get caught up in our plastic world that you lose the innocence and trust of a child. I always remember though, that whenever I said I couldn't do anything, such as playing a tune on the piano or my Maths homework, my Uncle Arthur used to say, "There's no such word as can't." I remember wondering what he was on about as I didn't realise at the time how very wise those words were, but I have never forgotten them.

As I became a teenager, the 'scary stuff' seemed to stop which I was thankful for. I was a typical teenager going out with my friends to discos and ice-skating rinks. As I grew older, the clairvoyant side of my abilities grew and my friends had started to cotton on to this. I became a kind of guru with the 'phone ringing constantly as people rang me for spiritual guidance. How did I know what the future held for these people? Well, later on in my life I was about to find out......

"When you follow your bliss, doors will open where you would not have thought there would be doors; and where there wouldn't be a door for anyone else."

—JOSEPH CAMPBELL

Throughout our paths in life we meet all kinds of people, some who turn out to be negative, to put it mildly. My life was no exception, and without naming those people (they will know who they are) I have, with a lot of heartache, broken the ties with them, be it relationships or friendships.

At the age of twenty I got married and we tried more or less straight away to have a family. It wasn't until five years later after many uncomfortable operations and procedures that I found out that I was pregnant at last. My husband liked to drink, and once I'd had the baby he started to go out more and more. I was stuck in the house with a newborn and for someone like me who liked to socialise I often felt like climbing the walls out of frustration and boredom. This made me feel guilty though when I looked at my baby daughter's little face. I felt so blessed to have a child that I pushed my loneliness to the back of my mind and threw myself into motherhood. My husband and I started to drift apart and we disagreed about many things, but we stayed together for the sake of our daughter. However, several years later when our daughter was around eight years of age, we were arguing yet again. I wanted him to spend more time with us as a family and he wanted to go out drinking with his mates. No-one would believe that this mild-mannered man who was so polite with everyone would turn into a monster after a drinking spree and I used to dread him coming home. The saying 'You never know what goes on behind closed doors' is so true and I was in the middle of a living nightmare which I thought would never end. I was certainly not prepared for what happened next.

I had a good friend who used to come to see me regularly with her two small children and as my husband and I drifted further apart, I confided in her as I needed someone to talk to about my heartache. It wasn't long before she started making excuses as to why she couldn't come round, and with every passing day my husband became more distant. Nothing I tried seemed to work and although I was distraught about the situation I said nothing to my family as I didn't want to upset them. My husband and I even went to Relate to try to work through our problems but an irretrievable breakdown had already occurred and there was nothing and no-one that could fix it. I remember my Mum telling me that my Dad had commented to her how I looked so sad all the time and I wasn't the bubbly person that I normally was.

Everything came to a head one day when I was at work. I was thinking about my friend and wondering why she didn't come round to see me anymore. Something felt wrong and a message popped into my head telling me to ring her. I went into an empty office, picked up the `phone and dialled her number. As her `phone was engaged, I rang our house to check that my husband was going out so I could have a girlie chat with my friend. Our `phone was also engaged. After about five minutes ringing both numbers, the penny finally dropped and I realised they were on the `phone to each other. My heart lurched and my head started pounding. I knew in that instant that he had become distant with me as he was seeing her. I ran in to my boss and said I'd got a family emergency and had to get home. As I ran in through the door I screamed out to him that I knew he was seeing my friend. He denied it but his face gave the game away, his expression riddled with guilt. I knew my instincts were right – they had been seeing each other behind my back. It was one of the dark periods of my life and I can't even find the words to describe how I felt after that double betrayal. Even though my husband denied anything went on, he said he just needed "someone to talk to." It has taken me years finally to send forgiveness out to both of them.

Several years later I married again and my new husband was a true 'Jack the lad'. He was a few years younger than me and was like a breath of fresh air. He had me in fits of laughter at his jokes (not *all* good!) and he took me and my daughter Lauren camping. He had a speedboat and we enjoyed crashing across the waves at Shell Island in Wales and driving into Barmouth when the tide allowed. However, this honeymoon period didn't last for long and it didn't take a genius to realise that I'd married him on the rebound. I didn't like the company he was starting to keep and he was pumping iron at the gym most evenings. What I didn't realise at the time was that he had started to take steroids and his temper got worse and worse. He really frightened me at times and one of the worst incidents occurred one evening when my daughter was staying over at her Dad's house.

My husband and I had been at a party and he was shouting and screaming at me accusing me (wrongly) of flirting with another man. He then proceeded to rip a picture off the wall and break it over his knee. He picked a table up and I thought he was going to throw it at me but instead he threw it - and what was left of the picture - into the garden. All of this was accompanied by foul expletives for all our neighbours to hear. He then punched the wall and furiously spun round and lunged at me. I turned and ran as fast as I could up the stairs and into the bathroom where I locked myself in. Thankfully, when he pursued me, he couldn't get into the room. He asked me to forgive him and, as I loved him, I gave him another chance.

A few weeks later when I went into work I heard the devastating news that a friend of mine had been rushed into hospital, having collapsed at work with an aneurism. A mutual friend and I were beside ourselves with worry and we both prayed long and hard. When the news came that she had died, we were both devastated. She was a beautiful soul, always there for others, and had her whole life ahead of her. It seemed so unfair and such an awful shock.

A few days later my friend and I went straight from work to order a wreath for the funeral. I had been trying to get hold of my husband to tell him I would be home late, to no avail. I didn't think there was anything amiss when I walked into the house an hour later. He shouted hello and I went upstairs to have a shower and put my nightdress on. However, when I came downstairs he was still standing in the kitchen, looking rigid with his back to me. My stomach sank. I tried to talk to him about choosing a beautiful wreath for my friend's funeral but when he turned to me his face was distorted with fury. Through gritted teeth he said, "I'm a growing lad and there was no tea for me when I came in. THIS is all I've had." He grabbed me round the neck and forced my head down over the kitchen unit. He threw a banana down onto the unit and opened a can of beans which he also emptied all over the unit. He wouldn't listen to a word I tried to say and I was absolutely terrified. He went over to the wall and punched it. Seeing my escape, I ran up the stairs and locked myself into the bathroom again. This is when I shouted out to the angels to help me find the strength to end the relationship. I thanked God that my daughter hadn't been in the house at the time to witness that awful scene. That must have been one of the darkest times of my life but after several moments I felt a warm feeling of calm wash over me and there is no other way to describe it than to say my soul felt lifted. I made the decision there and then to cut the ties with my destructive marriage and once again go it alone.

With two failed marriages behind me and being a single parent, I didn't think things could get any worse. But they did, when I began to get bullied at work. However, the person concerned was well respected and in a position of authority so when I originally spoke out, nobody believed me. Initially certain people started to turn against me and it was then that I did most of my praying to the angels and spirit to help me. I was telling the truth but no-one was listening so I decided to keep a diary of the incidents of bullying behaviour and the relevant dates and times. The atmosphere in the office was dreadful so I started looking round for another job. Ironically, once I sought the advice of the union, other people came forward to say they too had been bullied but were too scared to say anything. Not long afterwards I left and started a new job. A fresh start, once again!

Believe it or not, through each and every trauma I have come through the other side feeling stronger and more determined to surround myself with positive loving and trustworthy people. Although these relationships did not work out, I truly believe that they were meant to happen and I became resilient and determined not to make the same mistakes in the future. These are what I call 'life's little detours'. Just think about it: when a marriage or relationship breaks down there is often a lot of hurt and anger. If you are still holding on to the negative feelings around that person or situation, you won't be able to move on. What has to happen, and this isn't easy, is to send out forgiveness that will assist them in their own personal growth as well as your own. When you do this and truly mean it, you will find that you can move on in your own life and enjoy the company of new people who can now enter your life.

"Minds are like flowers, they only open when the time is right."

—STEPHEN RICHARDS

Cosmic ordering is asking the universe for what you want out of life. It's as simple as that. A good friend suggested that I try it but said that I must believe that my request would come to fruition.

I forgot about the conversation until a few months later, around November time when I was lamenting with a neighbour about how I never meet the right type of man. Her little son was playing with his toys on the floor by our feet and before I went home I asked him if he had written to Father Christmas yet. He replied that yes, he had, but he asked why I didn't do the same. I was surprised at this and said I wasn't sure what I wanted Father Christmas to bring me, but the little one was adamant and said, "Yes you do, you told Mummy that you wanted a new man! All you have to do is be good, and ask Father Christmas for a new man and he will make your wish come true." So I did exactly that! I wrote in detail about what I wanted my new man to look like and how he would treat me and that, more than anything, he must be spiritual. And while I was at it, I decided to ask the universe for another order. No matter which job I worked in, I wasn't truly happy as I knew my true purpose in life wasn't working in an office.

I gave it my best shot: "Dear Universe, I hope you don't think I am being cheeky putting in more than one order, but I know I am meant to be in a job that fulfils me and helps other people. I feel deep within my soul that I am meant to live a more spiritual life and that I will share my knowledge with others. Please help me to find my dream job doing something I love with every fibre of my being. I know you will help to guide me along the way. I believe 100% that you will honour my request. Lots of love, from Alison."

There, you don't get if you don't ask! I put my written requests in my Chinese 'wish-pot' knowing they would come to fruition.

"Letting go doesn't mean giving up, it means moving on."

—ANONYMOUS

Holding on to negative emotions from the past can stay with you for the rest of your life and can stop you from moving onward and upwards. Life is an adventure, but if you are at a stalemate you may never experience wonderful events to come. From personal experience, I have learned to send love and forgiveness to people or events that have caused me much pain. I am not saying it's easy! Over the years I have held on to stuff that became bigger baggage than I felt I could handle. However, eventually I was able to move on when I had decided that enough was enough and that I deserved better.

Not long after my marriage ended, my good friend Pam asked me along to a psychic circle she had joined in Warrington. During the evening we were sitting in a large circle and the teacher was holding some sealed envelopes in his hand. He explained that there was a different picture in each envelope and he handed one out to each of us. We were guided through a group meditation and the teacher asked us to focus on what was in the envelope. We were informed that our respective spirit guides would be working with us, and they would give us an image of what was depicted inside the envelope. We were then asked to give our envelope to the person sitting on our left and this person would open it. As Pam was sitting on my left, I handed her my envelope and the teacher went round each person in turn asking what images they were shown in the meditation.

When it was my turn, Pam opened my envelope and I remember feeling very nervous. My stomach had been gradually sinking as I heard what others had said, as they were sharing elaborate accounts of seeing lots of colours and bright lights. I didn't get anything like that. All I could see in my mind's eye was a small girl wearing a hat and standing by a tree. I shared this vision with everyone present and Pam was asked to tell everyone in the room what the picture was. When she said, "A small girl in a hat standing by a tree" and held the picture up for all to see, I couldn't believe it. Everyone in the room clapped and I remember thinking, "That was strange, it must have been beginners' luck." I know differently now, of course!

ENDING AND BEGINNING

"There are nights when the wolves are silent and only the moon howls."

—George Carlin

Not long after attending the psychic circle, I started to experience psychic activity such as anything electrical reacting when I was in a room. My boss told me to get out of her office one day when her lamp turned itself off. She actually told me I was weird, and asked if I was a witch!

Being at home was no different and there were often sounds of 'bumps in the night'. This happened so often that certain unexplained activity had almost become a second nature to me. Examples of this were lights turning up and down on their own, and the television turning itself on and off. Music would also blare out from my CD player, making both myself and my teenage daughter jump out of our skins. I started to read books on paranormal activity; I suppose I was looking for answers or any logical explanation as to why these strange things were happening around me.

One evening when my daughter was at her Dad's house, I asked a medium to come to the house to do readings for myself and a few of my friends. We were all excited and giggly after a few glasses of wine and we took it in turns to go and have our respective readings. I was the last one to go into the kitchen where the clairvoyant had set herself up. I remember feeling a little scared but when the reading started she took ages as she was looking up the messages in a book. It turned out she was only just starting off as a clairvoyant and we were the first people she had been to. I felt really disappointed, thinking, "I could do so much better at this myself." Nothing she gave me was right and when she had gone and I spoke to my friends they said, "Alison, you should do this – you always get everything right for us. Why don't you learn how to develop your gift?" After everyone had gone home, I started to clean up when I heard something drop from the ceiling and I saw sparks on the carpet. I jumped, my heart thumping hard in my chest. It was a light bulb that had thrown itself from the socket and landed on the floor - but why? I felt that someone from 'the other side' was trying to communicate with me but I didn't know what to do about it.

A few weeks later, Lauren and I were in the house together. Lauren was around fifteen years of age at the time and was upstairs in bed. I was relaxing downstairs watching the television after a hard day at work. Just as it got to a crucial part in the film I was watching I heard a crash from upstairs followed by a blood-curdling scream; I jumped up with a start, leapt up the stairs and ran into her bedroom. She was huddled up at the end of the bed and trembling. She pointed to the wall where two pictures had been and then to the floor where I saw them facing down. Miraculously they hadn't broken. Lying on top of them was a framed picture of her Granddad which had been on a shelf by her bed. She said she didn't see the pictures falling off the wall, she just heard the crash and saw them on the floor, but she watched as the picture of her Granddad had wobbled and toppled over to join the others. I settled her down and said there must have been a sudden breeze, but as I said it I realised that all the windows were shut. I told her not to worry, that she could sleep with the light on and I would be up to check on her at regular intervals.

When I came downstairs, I pondered over how those pictures and the photograph fell to the floor. It would be impossible unless someone knocked them off. What was going on? Why were we experiencing this paranormal activity? It crossed my mind that maybe someone was trying to tell me that my daughter also had the 'gift' and I thought back to an incident from a number of years ago that had always puzzled me. Here's what happened.

When Lauren was a toddler I had become an Avon representative and had put some books through the doors of prospective customers. A week later I had approached a large house in my area with a view to picking up my Avon book, hoping this particular customer had put an order in. As I was pushing Lauren in her pram along the path leading to the house she piped up, "Margaret lives here, and she has been painting." I stooped down to ask my little daughter what she had said in case I had misheard her, but she repeated the sentence word for word. I thought it was a very odd thing for a two-year old to say! I carried on along the path and knocked on the door. A woman opened it and said, "I've put a little order in, sorry I can't ask you in, but we've been painting." I felt a shiver run down my spine... As I came away I just had to see what she had ordered and was astonished when I saw her first name – Margaret!

I have related this story to many people over the years. My daughter is grown up now with three beautiful daughters of her own. She has had numerous experiences of premonitions herself over the years but I will never forget that little voice speaking with such conviction about something she could have known nothing about.

"The secret of health for both mind and body is not to mourn for the past, worry about the future or anticipate troubles, but to live in the present moment wisely and earnestly."

—THE BUDDHA

What helped to keep my sanity was being introduced to Reiki, which is a natural form of universal healing. The practitioner places their hands on the recipient's chakra points, starting at the crown chakra (top of the head) and ending up at the feet. Reiki is a gentle and non-intrusive complementary form of healing helping to balance the body by working on four levels of existence: the physical, psychological, emotional and spiritual. As a recipient you will feel relaxed as energy flows through your body. Everyone is different and some people will fall asleep, whereas others may feel emotional as old deep-rooted emotions rise to the surface. This is perfectly normal, as it's the body's natural ability to heal itself.

The first time I had a treatment was at Pam's house and I was lying on the bed in her bedroom. As she started the treatment, I felt tingly and could feel the warmth of her hands as she worked her way down each of my chakras. After the treatment I felt some sort of a release and I was extremely emotional. Pam said that this was normal as she had unblocked my chakras and the negative emotions I was holding on to had to be released otherwise I would become ill. It felt like waves of emotion were flowing through me from the top of my head to the bottom of my feet. I felt more relaxed than I had for a long time and decided I liked this treatment and I wanted more.

During my second treatment Pam suggested that I visualise a special place. It didn't take long before an image started to form in my mind's eye. I kept seeing part of a beach and then a lovely garden with brightly coloured flowers. I saw tropical fish and I realised that what I could see, smell, hear and sense was not in this country. The sun was really hot and the flowers in the garden were large brightly coloured exotic flowers. On the beach I could see the sand glistening and hear the sounds of the waves. The next thing I saw was an archway of exotic flowers and I realised that there was a dark-haired man by my side although I couldn't see his features. We walked through the archway together and I felt serene and at peace with the world. I knew that I had been given a snippet of something in my own future. When I discussed this with Pam, she too had seen the tropical fish. Who was this man?

As time went on, I had a burning desire to help others experience the wonders of Reiki healing. Pam attuned me to First Degree Reiki and that day will be imprinted on my brain forever. I remember thinking, why didn't I do this before? The sense of peace and oneness that I felt with each initiation is difficult to put into words. There are four initiations in First Degree Reiki and I felt the Reiki energy built up throughout my body. My hands were tingling and I saw beautiful colours swirling around as well as a sense of wellbeing that I had never experienced in my life before. I did my twenty-eight days of self-healing, which was amazing, and even though I was so relaxed that I often fell asleep, I had feelings of pure love emanating from my body. When I started to practise healing sessions on family and close friends I received some wonderful feedback. With experience I learned to go with the flow of the healing energy and my hands instinctively knew which parts of the body needed the healing the most. What was even more amazing was that I started to receive messages for the recipient such as name and places, and although I wondered at the time where this information was coming from, when I passed it onto the recipient they were able to confirm that the message was for them. They loved it as they were receiving a free Reiki treatment and a reading rolled into one!

I went on to be attuned to Second Degree where I learned the meanings and uses of the Reiki symbols and how to send distant healing to others. I sent healing to my past as I benefitted from the natural healing. People commented on how I seemed to glow and I realised how I was ceasing to worry about things so much, being happy to let things happen rather than trying to make them happen. I literally felt like my life was on the up. The icing on the cake came when I was attuned to Master level when I learned the final master symbol of Reiki. I knew that I would teach others about the wonders of Reiki, and I could finally recognise how my true life path was beginning to unfold before my very eyes. There is a saying that 'When the student is ready the teacher appears', and this was typical of being a Reiki Master Teacher. I have now attuned many students to the beautiful Reiki ray, and some of them in turn have gone on to teach too. Many clients have written to me thanking me for introducing them to Reiki and helping them to make positive changes in their lifestyle or their career.

Here are a few accounts of what people said about receiving a Reiki treatment for the first time (names have been changed to protect their privacy).

David

"The pain in my right shoulder had been recurrent for some time. The doctor had stated it was 'old age' creeping on, at which I was not amused! On recommendation from my wife, I asked Alison for a Reiki treatment. I found the experience extremely relaxing and actually fell asleep during the treatment. Throughout my treatments Alison gave me names of close loved ones who have passed over. My shoulder is not as painful as it was initially, and I will be asking Alison for further treatments in the near future."

Sandra

"At a time in my life when I was very emotionally upset, I approached Alison for a Reiki treatment. She provided both direct and distant healing to support me through my difficult time. During my treatment I felt relaxed and imagined taking myself to a peaceful spot where I could relax in tranquillity. I doubt whether I could have recovered without the inward healing that Reiki brought into my life."

Rebecca

"I had a Reiki treatment from Alison following the loss of my baby and suffering an ectopic pregnancy. Both events had left me feeling emotionally and physically drained. I found the treatment very relaxing, calming yet uplifting. I felt like my body was weightless, as if I were floating. I could feel heat from Alison's hands even when they were not physically upon me.

"I left my treatment feeling happy and with a clear mind and had the best night's sleep afterwards, which I hadn't had in so long.

"I had a subsequent Reiki treatment from Alison when I was pregnant with my son who is now eight months old. Alison said she could hear a baby giggling when she put her hands over my tummy and felt a strong presence in the room at the time of my treatment.

"The strangest thing was that when I was receiving my treatment I saw an image of an angel with a green light around him and although I didn't mention what I saw to Alison, she told me after she had finished my treatment that she had asked Archangel Raphael to assist with my healing and that he surrounded me in a green light. I will never forget that image and how relaxed and peaceful I felt after receiving Reiki from Alison."

"We do not create our destiny, we participate in its unfolding. Synchronicity works as a catalyst toward the working out of that destiny."

—DAVID RICHO, THE POWER OF COINCIDENCE

It's not every day that a book helps to change your life, but that's exactly what James Redfield's book The Celestine Prophecy did for me. The book is about the insights and coincidences of life and discovering who we are and where humans fit into the wonders of the universe. There is an energy field or aura around every living thing, from people to animals and plants. Our energy field should stay intact, but once someone steps inside our personal space or aura they can then start to sap us of our energy and gain control. How many times has this happened to you, where someone has left you feeling drained, angry or upset?

The Celestine Prophecy teaches us how to understand the new spiritual awareness by living in the here and now, and being grateful for the wonderful things in our lives. In doing so, our vibrations are raised to a height where the ego doesn't exist. This is when 'coincidences' start to occur, which are synchronistic events that our spirit guides and angels put on our life path to make us sit up and notice. These signs can present themselves in many ways, such as thinking about a friend you haven't seen for a long time then bumping into them, or a chance meeting with someone new who can help to open new doors for you.

One of the first synchronistic events that happened in my life was how I came to read The Celestine Prophecy in the first place. I heard about it initially at a yoga class when our teacher asked if I had read it. I hadn't even heard of the book at that time so I never gave it a second thought until Pam recommended it to me. She said she'd read it and it made so much sense to her about life in general, but I still resisted.

A few days later I was talking to another friend about a particular subject when she turned the conversation around to The Celestine Prophecy. I can't even remember how it came into the conversation when we had been talking about something entirely different, but I do remember looking up to the sky and saying "You win!" not knowing exactly who I was addressing!

Around this time I started to see angels everywhere - when I turned the television on, in shops, or hearing songs on the radio with the word angel being prominent. Every time I saw these signs I knew without a doubt that it was from the celestial realms as I had a deep feeling of peace from within. I knew that angels were communicating with me, but I didn't know what to do about it.

One morning I got up, opened the door and there on the doorstep was a beautiful pure white feather. It was a blustery day and yet the feather stayed there long enough for me to see it. I thought back to my request to Father Christmas where I'd asked him for a new man, and I had to laugh to myself. Were the angels guiding someone special into my life? As this thought popped into my head I felt warm and comforted.

Reading The Celestine Prophecy had opened up a new world for me and I knew that most of the questions I had lay within my soul. All I had to do was to unlock them and I started to feel very excited about the adventure that was about to unfold. A couple of weeks later I was cleaning my bookcase and cataloguing my books when a book seemed to leap off the shelf and land by my feet. As I bent down to pick the book up, I saw the title Healing With the Angels. The celestial realms were trying to give me a message – but what was it?

Later that week I was inwardly asking the angels if I was doing the right thing about a particular event in my life. As I looked out of the window, I saw the most amazing sight and I had to look twice. It was a cloud formation of an angel with outstretched wings. If that wasn't definitive confirmation that I was doing the right thing, I don't know what was.

"In helping others, we shall help ourselves, for whatever good we give out completes the circle and comes back to us."

—FLORA EDWARDS

Helping others gave me focus and I have always believed that what you give out, you get back. Even if I could help one person, I would have achieved something and it was better than nothing. As I started to get my strength back, I felt like a renewed spirit who had come home to roost and I started to talk to the angels asking them for help and guidance for myself and others. I knew they were calling out to me and wanted me to spread their love and light to others, but I have to admit I was getting quite impatient and wondered how or when I would find out my destiny.

More and more people came to me for advice and it hurt me to see people in pain. One example of this is a friend of mine who at the time was in a destructive relationship. It was awful to see how much weight she had lost as well as losing her confidence and vibrant personality. She spent endless hours on the `phone describing what was going on as I listened. The only advice I could give her was that it would accumulate and come to a head in the form of a catalyst where she would have to make a decision. Although I said she should get out of the relationship, I couldn't live her life for her and the decision had to be hers.

A few weeks later we were having coffee together at my house and chatting away as usual. Everything was nice and relaxed until her `phone rang; it was him. I saw her jump up as if to stand to attention and she mumbled that she had to go and pick him up. She looked pale, her eyes wide and frightened. At that point I don't know what came over me, but witnessing one of my best friends letting someone control them and seeing her deteriorating every day caused the anger to bubble up inside me. I went over to her and held her hands, asking her if she trusted me, to which she nodded. I said I was about to tell her something that would hurt her initially but in the future she would thank me for. I then told her that she had to leave him. I gave her information around him that had come from a trustworthy source, and reassured her that she was going to meet someone else in the future.

I told her that she would meet this person and that he would have links to the police, although I knew he didn't work there. I went on to say that he would treat her how she deserved to be treated and that she would be very happy. However, this would only happen if she was willing to cut the ties with her existing relationship and move forward in her life. I said that she had to be strong, but I would help her in any way I could. I wanted to shake some sense into her but my heart ached to see her looking so frail and bewildered. She trusted me implicitly and she knew I was telling the truth. We hugged and she left.

After she had gone, my head was saying, "Where did all that information come from?" I also thought "Oh no, what have you done? You could destroy your wonderful friendship" but my heart and my gut feeling were saying, "She is going to move on at last." Well, my heart and gut feeling won. My friend found the strength to sever the relationship and although at times she wondered if she had done the right thing, I could see her blossoming before my very eyes and getting back her independence, gaining weight and being the bright soul that she always was.

Oh, and the guy I saw her with in the future? Yes, everything I told her came to fruition and they are happily married. He used to be a police officer in the traffic department and was introduced to her by a friend who worked with her at the police station. He is a fabulous friend, a wonderful husband to her, and he treats her like a queen. Exactly how she deserves to be treated!

CHAPTER 2

Spirit Guides

"Love is a symbol of eternity. It wipes out all sense of time, destroying all memory of a beginning and all fear of an end."

—ANONYMOUS

Since my divorce I had been on many dates but had not met anyone that I felt I had anything in common with and I resigned myself to the fact that I would be on my own for some time. I missed the closeness of being in a relationship and to have someone to love and for them to love me back. It was coming up to Christmas time and our Christmas party at work. I worked as a civilian manager for the police and the party was being run by our CID team. There should have been me and three of my friends going to the party; despite not feeling well, there was something spurring me on to go to the party, so I went along with my friend Tracey.

During the evening I met John whom I felt really comfortable around and it was as if we had known each other forever. The strangest thing was that he wasn't going to come to the party either; he said that his friend was trying to persuade him to go with him, but he declined. However, he felt at the last minute that he had to attend so he rang his friend who accompanied him to the party. Apparently this was the first works Christmas party that John had had the inclination to attend. He said that something seemed to be urging him to go, as if he was being pushed by unseen hands. I dread to think how things would have turned out if we hadn't both gone to the party. This was definitely one of the most special synchronised events of my life. If either of us hadn't listened to that voice from within, we may not have met and it could have been a 'sliding doors' moment where our respective lives would have taken on a different course entirely. Father Christmas certainly came early that year!

John and I started dating and we got engaged a year later, eventually getting married in Margarita. As I was looking through our wedding album I felt tingly all over because as I held a photograph of the two of us on the beach, I realised that I recognised it. I had 'seen' that beach when Pam had given me the Reiki treatment. It was exactly the same, down to two deck chairs under a tree and parasols further down the beach. What was uncanny was looking at the photograph of us getting married in the gardens of the hotel. It shows John and me walking underneath an archway of flowers exactly the same as in my vision, and the fish I had seen were the tropical fish native to the island. I'd had a premonition of my wedding to the man of my dreams and that was only the beginning!

"Why not move into your house bringing joy into every crevice? For you are the secret treasure-bearer and always have been. Didn't you know?"

—RUMI

I sold my house in Runcorn and moved into John's house in Northwich, taking my 'baggage' with me – my daughter, cat and dog – and it didn't take long for us all to settle into our new home. Everything about John, the move and the house itself, felt right. It was a beautiful house with a lovely garden and my daughter enrolled for college in Northwich and got a little job as a waitress in our local country pub.

Not long after we'd moved in I passed my driving test at the age of 41! As a single mum for many years I wasn't able to afford lessons so they had to go on the backburner whilst I tried to keep a roof over our heads, working long hours and paying the mortgage and bills. However, now that things had changed and there were two wages coming into the house life couldn't have been better. I still felt that there was something missing and although my home life was happy, I felt that working in an office wasn't for me anymore. I silently asked the universe for help.

One particular evening John was working a night shift at the police station. I was in bed and was exhausted; I must have fallen asleep as soon as my head hit the pillow. My daughter was staying over at her father's house so apart from the dog and the cat I was alone in the house. I awoke with a start and wondered what had woken me. I couldn't hear anything and the room was pitch black, but I could see the light of the alarm clock which said 2.30 a.m.

All of a sudden, the bed starting shaking on its own. I could feel my heart banging away in my chest and my hands felt clammy as the bed continued to shake. As it was so dark I couldn't see anyone or anything so I screamed out, "Leave me alone, go away, you're frightening me," and the bed stopped shaking as quickly as it had started.

My heart pounded away and I was rooted to the spot. What the hell was that? I called the dog into the room and cuddled up with her all night with the light on. Was this someone just trying to attract my attention or did they mean me harm? I really didn't know, but made up my mind there and then to seek out a psychic circle so I could hopefully deal with whatever it was in the right way.

More unexplained things happened over the next few months such as hearing whispers, but there was no-one there, feeling someone touching me, and as before lights turning themselves up and down on their own. I kept hearing someone calling my name softly but it must have been a disembodied voice as I couldn't see anyone.

Another strange incident occurred when I was at my friend Tracey's house. We were sitting talking when all of a sudden her television switched itself on. I was used to this in my own house but not in anyone else's; I knew it had to have something to do with me. She asked me to stop messing about and asked me to give her the remote control. However the words stuck in her mouth when she could see the remote was on a table on the other side of the room. She said, "Al, it's you! These things only happen when you're around – how do you do that?" The thing was, I just didn't know.

"Stop the words now. Open the window in the centre of your chest and let the spirits fly in and out."

—RUMI

Flicking through our local newspaper, an advertisement caught my eye. A lady called Jackie Dennison and her business partner at the time were advertising psychic development places at a place called Feathers in our local town. I rang up and enquired about the course and said I wanted to be considered for a place. They took my details and rang back to say I had a place booked on the course in three months time. However in the meantime I was informed that they were holding a spiritual weekend with a guest speaker from Gibraltar. She said that the gentleman, Joey Martinez, had done weekend workshops for them before and that he would be doing one called Working With Higher Energies. There were a couple of places left if I was interested! I spoke to John who told me to go and enjoy it, so I rang back and confirmed my place.

During the morning of the workshop I was sitting at home in the conservatory with John wondering if I was doing the right thing by attending, when I felt a soft breeze around me. John had felt it too and we wondered who it could be. I then had a vision of my Grandma (my father's mother) wagging her fingers at me! I knew she was telling me not to be so silly and that I should go on the workshop.

Later that day I attended the workshop. The building was an old cottage, really quaint, with the original fireplace still in situ and with winding stairs. As I had moved house into a different town I didn't know any of the other people who were on the workshop, but it didn't matter. They all seemed really nice and we soon got chatting. Eventually we were asked to get into pairs to do one of the practical exercises. This particular one was healing one's aura and I was with a Scottish girl called Sally (name changed). As I held my hands over Sally's head I could feel my hands start to tingle as the healing emanated through her crown chakra. I could feel a pair of eyes on me and I looked up to see Joey intent on what I was doing. He smiled at me and came over. He said to me that he felt I had a lot to give, but not to try too hard as the gift that I had was natural. These words are some of the wisest I have heard and I will never forget them. Joey and I became firm friends and a few years after our initial meeting he came over from Gibraltar for me to attune him as a Reiki Master.

When I attended the psychic development course a few weeks later, I recognised a couple of faces from Joey's workshop and it wasn't long before I got to know everyone in my group. I couldn't wait for each week to learn more about developing my gift. One of the first things that Jackie taught us was how to ground and put psychic protection around ourselves, which is imperative when working with spirit energy.

Each week we enjoyed a guided meditation and afterwards we had to share what we had experienced with the group. It became evident that a couple of the people present felt they were better than everyone else and I started to compare what information I'd got in the meditation with others. This is the first mistake I made and when I am giving talks now it is one of the first things I will highlight. Never, ever, compare yourself with others. This beautiful quote by Pierre Teilhard de Chardin says it all: "We are not human beings having a spiritual experience, we are spiritual beings having a human experience."

Your spirit guide will develop you at a pace that is right for you. Eventually I learned to trust and believe in what I was being given and felt so humble when loved ones I had lost to spirit came to join me in meditation.

By this time I had got used to feeling my spirit guide around me. Initially I would feel warm, which was then followed by a cool breeze coming in from the left and then the feeling of someone standing behind me in a protective way. Eventually, once I had gained confidence in my own abilities I really enjoyed developing my gift. There were a few events that I will never forget when being part of the psychic circle but what you are about to read is the most amazing.

"I feel the love of my special friend - the silent one who's by my side to love and cherish, to listen and guide."

—A WYNNE-RYDER

During one of our meditations we had to step into a boat, and although I can't remember everything now about that meditation there is one thing that is imprinted on my brain. As I got off the boat, a man came over and handed me an embroidered handkerchief with the initial 'M' on it. I wondered about this and couldn't concentrate for a while, but then I could see the outline of a lady. I saw her face fairly clearly, but couldn't see the rest of her properly. As I approached her she smiled and said to me, "This is my best side, I was lovely once, you know." I would put her around sixty years of age although I could have been way out – I was never good with estimating ages. I could see that she had been really attractive in her day and I asked her what her name was. Her reply was, "Maria Hedley." She said, "I think you have something of mine," and when I looked down I realised that I was still holding the handkerchief that the man had given to me. I handed it to her and she waved as she walked away clutching the handkerchief.

Everything about this meditation was so clear, vivid and precise. It was the first time I had ever been given someone's full name. When sharing my meditation with the group, Jackie said I should do some research and look up Maria Hedley to find out who she was. The next evening, I did a few Google searches and, just when I was about to give up, I came across her. Maria Hedley had married James Leathart (1820 – 1895) who was a Newcastle lead manufacturer and was known to have one of the largest art collections in his time. In 1862 he commissioned Dante Gabriel Rossetti to paint Maria and the finished painting was produced on December 25th, 1862. I couldn't believe my eyes when I saw the painting of Maria, as it was the lady I had seen in my meditation. She was younger in the painting but there was no mistaking those eyes. Her portrait was beautiful, and I re-membered that she'd said, "This is my best side." She had posed as a model for Rossetti who was part of the pre-Raphaelite brotherhood.

The portrait is one of Rossetti's masterpieces and it started to make sense as to why I have always been drawn to pre-Raphaelite art. But why did Maria appear to me in my meditation? I knew in my heart that eventually I would find out and I started to feel very, very excited.

"Meditation is the soul's perspective glass."

—OWEN FELTHAM

It came to the time (which it had to eventually!) where we would do some psychic art. I have never been able to draw and I knew this would be something I would struggle with but I decided to go for it and do my best. We started off gently and Jackie did a drawing and put it into a sealed envelope. We had to link in with her inwardly and draw what was inside the envelope. I drew a colourful butterfly that had little bobbles on the tips of its wings. My heart dropped when Jackie opened the envelope and showed us that she had drawn a dream catcher. None of us got it right, but at least we'd had a go. All of a sudden, one of the girls in our circle said, "Ali, you know that gorgeous bracelet of yours that John bought you – the one with the dream catchers hanging off it? When you get home, look inside one of the little dream catchers. I saw a butterfly just like that on it when you had the bracelet on the other day." As soon as I got home I took the bracelet out of my jewellery box and there it was, the butterfly as I had drawn it (albeit quite badly), with the same shaped wings together with bobbles, inside one of the dream catchers. Wow!

"I know you are with me every day inspiring me and leading the way."

—A WYNNE-RYDER

In our psychic development class a few of the people in our circle had 'met' their spirit guides and even seemed to know their names. I felt quite frustrated as although I could feel my guide around me, I hadn't seen him. I felt my guide was male because I kept hearing a male voice calling my name. However, all I could see of him in my meditations was part of a sleeve.

A few months into the course I had a strange dream where I was part of our psychic development circle but the only person I recognised was Jackie. I could see the faces of others present but I didn't know them. At the head of the circle, I could see a male who was sitting in the lotus position. He had long dark hair and a band around his head with a beautiful blue stone in the centre. He wore a long light-coloured robe. He beckoned me over and hugged me. No words were spoken, and the dream felt so real – I truly felt that I was there in the room with him and nothing else mattered. On waking up from the dream, I knew in my heart that I had met my spirit guide. A few weeks later, I was sitting on my swing in our garden when I felt his presence around me. I asked him his name, to which he replied Zamil. I asked where he was from and I heard the word Marrakesh. So my main spirit guide originated from Morocco. How wonderful! I felt blessed that he had wanted to share this information with me.

CHAPTER 3

The Audition

"Until one has loved an animal, a part of one's soul remains unawakened."

—Anatole France

When I moved into John's house in Northwich, which is now my home, both my cat Topsy and my little dog Jet had settled into their new home really well and I want to share a lovely memory I have about Topsy. After a couple of years living in the house we decided to get a puppy as a companion for Jet. We chose a female black Labrador as our new addition to the family and we called her Libby. She is one of the most lovable and gentle creatures I have ever had the privilege of meeting and even our cat Topsy, who wasn't one for cuddles or affection, absolutely loved Libby. She used to rub her head on Libby's big head every morning as a greeting and often curled up with her at night.

Over time I noticed that Topsy, who was now around fifteen years old, was getting very thin and frail. She was a very old lady, but she was eating and drinking and was happy, with her tail always in the air. Never a cat that you could pick up, she remained aloof with everyone apart from me. There was a total connection without words, a sort of telepathy that went on between us that, to be honest, neither my husband nor my daughter could understand. The day came when spirit told me she would be 'taken over the rainbow bridge'. I rang in to work and told them I wouldn't be in as my cat would be leaving this mortal world and luckily they knew me well. When my husband came down in his police uniform I still had my dressing gown on. He asked why I wasn't ready for work so I told him I wasn't going in as Topsy was going over to the rainbow bridge. He asked how I knew and I said I just did; although he stood there looking incredulous he knew better than to argue with me so he went off to work.

Not long after he had gone, Topsy lay down by the radiator in our living room. She felt cold so I put a soft blanket over her and knelt down beside her. She looked at me and raised her paws at me. I was so upset at losing my friend of fifteen years and asked the angels to help me. All of a sudden I felt a warm breeze around me and a sense of calm. I looked at Topsy who had laid her head down but was still looking at me and I talked to her softly giving her some Reiki as the angels took her gentle soul away. I saw glittery lights like stars over her body, and eventually she was gone. I was absolutely distraught, but thanked the angels for hearing my prayers, and I knew that she would be absolutely fine in her place of rest. After a while I realised I couldn't leave her body by the radiator so I picked her up gently and took her down the garden into my meditation room. I placed her on the carpet in the room and began to meditate.

What happened next startled me beyond belief. I heard a pattering on top of the summer house roof and then distinctly heard a cat mewing. My immediate thought was, "Oh my God, she isn't dead", and I leapt up from the chair and went over to her body – which was literally a shell now and of course it was completely still. I ran outside to see if there was another cat that had landed on the roof but there was nothing there. I truly believe that it was Topsy who had come to visit me one last time to let me know she was happy and pain-free.

I have felt her many times since and a few weeks ago I put a picture on Facebook of my little dog Jet who herself is now around sixteen years old. As I was in a rush after putting the photographs on, I didn't take much notice of them; but Jackie sent me a message saying, "Al, have you noticed the orb on Jet?" I took a good look at the picture and sure enough there it was. Was this Topsy getting in on the act? I would like to think so as I have felt her presence around me many times since she passed over, and I often feel her jumping on the bed even though I can't see her. Isn't it wonderful to know that our pets, who are part of our family and a big part of our lives, can still visit us in the same way that our family or friends in spirit can?

"Be yourself; everyone else is already taken."

—OSCAR WILDE

Jackie worked on a TV show in Canada called Rescue Mediums. This came about when she was doing her own family history and a distant relative gave her some information about her great uncle and his wife moving to Toronto, Canada. Jackie did some research and eventually found herself talking to Michael Lamport who was now living in the house that her great uncle had lived in many years before. Michael asked what Jackie did for a living and when she told him that she was a clairvoyant medium, he and his partner Gregory Sheppherd asked Jackie and her sister-in-law to meet them and they did a pilot for the show called Rescue Mediums. The rest is history!

In 2009 Jackie had received the fabulous news that Rescue Mediums had been renewed. The network was now looking for a new partner to co-host the show with Jackie. Auditions had already taken place in Canada, but now the director of the show and one of the cameramen had come over to film at Feathers. A few of us were asked if we would like to audition and of course we jumped at the chance. I decided to go along for the fun and experience of it.

The day of the auditions arrived and as it was a Sunday my family had come to our house for their lunch. It was a tradition and I was doing my usual thing of running around after everyone, so I didn't have time to 'doll myself up'. I scraped my hair up into a bun and grabbed something to wear from the wardrobe, telling my family I would be back in a couple of hours time.

Not long afterwards, I was standing outside the building in the pouring rain and wondering what I was thinking of. I rang my friend Joey in Gibraltar to ask if he felt I was doing the right thing. Joey calmed me down and told me just to be myself. I spoke to him for a while and just as we had finished our conversation one of the ladies who had auditioned came to unbolt the door. I could see that the three of them who were there were 'on a high' and had thoroughly enjoyed themselves. This made me feel better in an instant and I decided to go in and have fun. At that point I received a message from Zamil. He said, "Take your shoes off." I asked what he meant, but he just repeated the message.

Jackie came to greet me and introduced me to Gregory Shepherd, the director of Rescue Mediums, and one of the cameramen. They both seemed lovely down-to-earth people and I soon relaxed. I wasn't sure what I was supposed to do, so I followed Jackie upstairs. I was drawn to one of the rooms on the first floor. I went in, sat down, and Jackie came and sat down beside me. Greg and the cameraman were in front of us filming. I had already grounded, 'opened up' and put psychic protection around myself prior to coming into the building and I heard Zamil's voice again saying, "Take your shoes off." I said to Jackie, "Do you mind if I take my shoes off, as I feel more grounded that way?" She said, "No problem", although she looked rather bemused.

As soon as I took my shoes off, I closed my eyes and had a vision of a lovely lady dressed in black wearing a white pinafore. I then heard the song Mammy and could see a troupe of Black and White Minstrels. I felt a little embarrassed saying what I had got, but I told Jackie all the information and she smiled. She asked if I had got anything else from this lady; I closed my eyes again and focused. The lady continued to give me more information and was sending lots of love at the same time. Jackie started to look excited and as the lady gave me more information Jackie confirmed that she knew who the lady was. It was someone very special to Jackie and as her eyes welled with tears, we hugged each other and I felt a strong connection between the two of us. Once my audition had finished, I came back home again feeling 'on a high' as I had thoroughly enjoyed myself! Jackie rang me that evening to say how well I had done and how fabulous that her loved one had come through to me.

The next day in work I couldn't concentrate properly. I had known for a long time that I wanted to follow my spiritual path but the feeling was stronger than ever and I was beginning to feel totally dissatisfied with working in an office. I had seen a sparkle of what *really* working with spirit would be like and now I felt uneasy. My head was telling me to forget the audition as there would be no way I would get the role. After all, I had only gone to gain the experience and have fun, but I couldn't get away from how my heart kept leaping every time I thought about it and I felt really excited.

A couple of months later, I received a call at work from Jackie about the show. All seventeen auditions had been seen by the TV network in Canada and they had picked me as Jackie's new partner on the show! It took a while for the information to sink in, but when it did, I shouted "YES!" at the top of my voice. Apparently one of the people whom I worked with later said she thought I had won the lottery! As far as I was concerned, I had.

"Nothing is worth more than this day."

—JOHANN WOLFGANG VON GOETHE

One of the hardest things I had to do was tell my Mum what I would be doing. She has never believed in spirit and always said, "There are no such things as ghosts" and another of her sayings is, "The living will do you more harm than the dead will." So I found myself sitting on the settee opposite her at her house with a cup of tea in my hand. I told her I had something to say to her and she said, "Well, that sounds ominous." I told her not to worry and decided just to come out with it and tell her everything. She was silent for a while and then she said, "Are you happy?" and I said, "I am happier now than I have been for a long, long time." Her reply was, "Well, if you're happy, I'm happy." I knew in that instant that I'd received her blessing. What a shock it must have been for her!

"Our light is shining for you to see, have faith and we will do the rest."

—RUBY (MY SPIRIT GUIDE)

My month's notice at work was now up and I was having a couple of weeks at home before flying out to Canada. During this time I had felt a new spirit guide coming in. I kept sensing a female presence around me and she felt very gentle. I was also aware of someone standing behind Zamil in meditations and, when I asked who it was, he told me that a new guide was being brought forward to help me in my new role as a rescue medium. I then saw a lady step from behind him. She was lovely, with long red hair, a flowing white gown and a beautiful serene face. Her face looked vaguely familiar but I pushed that thought to the back of my head telling myself not to be so silly.

That evening, I had lost my engagement ring and couldn't understand how I could have been so careless. Three days later, I was searching for some hair clips in my bedside cabinet and when I opened the drawer something grabbed my attention. Whatever it was seemed to be glinting brightly in my face and I bent down to retrieve it. It was my engagement ring but the strange thing was that the diamonds were not shining brightly, only the ruby. I then got a vision of my new lady spirit guide in my third eye and I knew what she was telling me. Her name was Ruby. Well hello Ruby, I know we are going to have plenty of fun on our new adventure together!

"I am more than I appear to be; all the world's strength and power lies inside me."

—MANTRA USED BY SPIRITUAL LEADERS OF THE EAST

I had never been to Canada before and I think it sank in properly on my very first flight to start my new job. My heart kept skipping – what had I done? What if I don't come up to scratch, what if the crew don't like me, what if I get too homesick? It didn't take me too long to settle into the flight. Jackie and I nattered on and off, and I enjoyed some relaxing time reading and watching a movie. I remember at one point looking down and I saw a small gold star on my knee. It was one of those little paper stars and I hadn't a clue as to how it got there. I saw it as a 'welcome gift' from my spirit guides and I thanked them inwardly. It was much later on, and through succinct confirmation, that it was another new guide making herself known to me – Star!

When we landed, and after collecting our luggage, we had to queue up to pay for and obtain our work permits. Our producer Michael Lamport was picking us up from the airport with our production manager. They soon made me feel welcome by taking us for a drink before driving us to our suites in Toronto.

When we arrived at the building we were given two keys and we were shown to our allocated rooms. Our production manager put the keys behind her back and asked us to choose one. I was happy as I got the room I secretly wanted and Jackie appeared happy with her room too. When we had settled in properly I went over to her room to talk to her and said, "Oh, trust you to get this room, look who we have here..." It was a large ornamental flamingo hiding behind the curtains and she hadn't even seen it. We both laughed as one of Jackie's spirit guides always gives her the sign of the flamingo just as the new seasons of Rescue Mediums are about to start. Well, he didn't let her down, did he?

"There is no I in teamwork."

—ANONYMOUS

The first day after settling into our rooms and freshening up, our director Greg and producer Michael took Jackie and me to dinner, to welcome me to the show. Greg asked if there was anything I wasn't too sure of or confident about, and I mentioned that the only thing I had never done properly before is psychic art. I told him that I have never been able to draw and I did feel quite nervous about showing my stick men drawings on national TV! He said he would arrange a meeting with his lovely wife who is a children's author and illustrator. The next day, I found myself in her studio practising the basics of art. I felt much more comfortable afterwards although the proof would be in the pudding the first time I produced some psychic art.

The next trip was to the doctor to get checked over properly and ensure I was fit to do the job, and then it was back again to our apartments for a well-earned rest. The following day was meeting our dresser and I had a fabulous time – she was lovely and helped both Jackie and me to choose appropriate clothes for the show. The colours we wear have to co-ordinate as well as being comfortable because one outfit has to be worn for two consecutive days for continuity. Another thing that has to be taken into consideration is patterns on tops we wear. For instance, I couldn't wear a pink spotted top while Jackie wore a green striped one. Well we could, but we would look a garish spectacle in front of the television cameras.

The next day I met Edna, our head researcher who is lovely, making me feel like I had known her forever, and we soon became good friends. Edna has the unenviable job of finding out who it is that we have rescued, trawling through reams of archived documents such as birth certificates, marriage certificates and the census. We have to give our premonitions and psychic art to Edna before filming the reading of our premonitions to each other on air, as she has to type them all up and photocopy our drawings with a view to showing them to the respective homeowners.

I was quite apprehensive on the first day that I met the rest of the crew. I mean, they didn't know me from Adam, but I needn't have worried. They were all great and it didn't take long before they welcomed me into their fold. I was now part of the team.

CHAPTER 4

Going to the Light

"Every child is an artist; the problem is staying an artist when you grow up."

—PABLO PICASSO

Psychic art is a form of communication with spirit which is a wonderful and creative form of mediumship. People are now realising that you don't have to be a fantastic artist to practise in this way. All you have to do is trust in your spirit guide, let your inhibitions go, and just see what happens. Believe me, it works!

In a nutshell, it is making a sketch that our own spirit guides draw 'through us'. For me, this has been one of the most amazing things about being on the show, as it had been a standing joke when I was growing up that I could never draw while my sister Carol is an illustrator, graphic designer and fashion designer. Stick men are usually my forte!

To give you an idea of how my psychic art is carried out, I open up as usual to the spirit world and ask my drawing guide Ruby to work through me to give me clues as to what Jackie and I will find during our psychic investigation. My main aim when asking for this information is that we help the homeowners, as well as those poor souls who are stuck 'on a different vibration'. It is our job as rescue mediums to help them to reach their final destination by sending them towards the light. I rest my pencil on the page with these thoughts and Ruby draws through me. I never know what I am drawing until I see the finished product. Sometimes my drawings are done with my eyes shut, other times with them open, but they are always created with the right intention.

The drawings that Jackie and I produce for the show link together strongly therefore enabling us to uncover the mysteries behind the incidents occurring in the homes we visit. Each of my drawings is given a title which is indicative of the story that will eventually unfold.

I never doubt the information given to me by Ruby, who is my inspiration, and I feel honoured that she is working through me in such a unique way. This is a description of how I felt when doing psychic art for the very first time at the start of my first season and is an extract from notes I made at the time.

"I picked up my art pad and pencil, and asked my guide to draw through me and give me clues as to what we will experience when we start our investigation. Eventually, I felt the pencil moving and it was a very strange feeling, but as pressure was very gentle I thoroughly enjoyed the experience. When I had finished, I gave my drawing a title, dated it and put my signature on it." What was it? Well, I wasn't sure, but it looked like some kind of map. Since that very first time, I have done many psychic drawings, and they have become extremely accurate as I tend to draw clues as to what the story will be when it unfolds. I can't draw faces, so it's just as well that Jackie can, and I feel our drawings complement each other. Okay, so I will never be Rembrandt! But I am proud of what I can achieve in order to help the homeowners and the spirits stuck between two worlds.

One of our cameramen jokingly refers to me as "Pablo" and the crew love to see what Jackie and I have drawn. They know the location of the property whereas we know nothing and have to solely rely on premonitions and psychic art given to us as clues by our respective spirit guides. I love it when the crew gasps in wonder at what we have drawn.

One thing I have learned from the show is that you don't have to be a fabulous artist to do psychic drawings or artwork. Just put your trust in your spirit guide and enjoy seeing the finished product.

"If you hear a voice within you saying you cannot paint, by all means paint and that voice will be silenced."

—VINCENT VAN GOGH

An example of one of the drawings I did for the last season of the show is a drowning, which was a male spirit in turmoil whom we sent over to the light. Toys and balloons were more clues on one of my drawings, which led us to a certain area in the house where we did the rescue of a spirit child.

One episode was filmed at a caravan site and I drew a Pied Piper-type figure with children around him. This character turned out to be a male spirit who was protecting spirit children who were stuck between two worlds due to a portal that had been opened in the grounds of the caravan site because of the improper use of an ouija board. The male spirit assisted in sending those little ones over to the spirit world, and once this had been done we closed the portal.

For one of our earlier shows during my first season, I drew the Virgin Mary. As Jackie and I were walking around outside the property, we saw a statue of the Virgin Mary in the garden. A definite clue to our investigation. As the Virgin Mary statue was situated by the front door of the house, we walked through the front door into one of the bedrooms located opposite the door. It didn't take us long to deduce that that the bedroom belonged to the daughter of the homeowners, and it was she who had experienced most of the spiritual activity in the home.

As Jackie and I entered her bedroom, we were drawn to a picture over her bed that seemed to be glowing. It was a picture of the Virgin Mary. This crucial clue made us realise that the daughter's bedroom was the area where we needed to be, to ask the spirit to come forward and communicate with us, so we could help them over to the spirit world.

In order to send spirits to the 'other side', we have to send them to the light. When a person dies, a beautiful white light is sent down from the celestial realms. When that person walks into the light their angel will come forward to guide them to their loved ones who have already passed over.

However, some spirits will not walk towards the light as they feel they have unfinished business here on Earth. That is when they become 'stuck' between two worlds. Once the light goes back to the spirit world they cannot reach their destination until they are helped over by a medium specialising in rescue mediumship work.

We start the spirit rescue by filling each room in the house with bright white light. If relevant, we also include the immediate outside area of the property as well. Once we have done this, the entity or entities move within the light towards us. This works every time, whether the trapped spirit themselves are gentle or malevolent (Jackie and I have encountered a few of those along the way). They basically cannot 'escape' once this exercise is conducted, and as they get nearer we may feel, see, hear or sense them.

A good example was at one of the homes we were asked to investigate. The homeowners had been experiencing strong paranormal activity and during our investigation we had 'met' three entities. As they moved towards us within the light, we could see from their clothing that they were from the Victorian era. One seemed to be a 'helper', and the other two were a lady who died in immense physical pain and her son who had died of dementia. Both were stuck within the wrong vibration, or dimension, and for their own reasons had resisted walking towards the light at the point of death. Our helper was male and he felt quite different from the other two spirits as he had a strong but peaceful energy around him. With the other two we felt disorientated and in a lot of pain as they proceeded to put physical conditions on us, such as stabbing pains, headaches and feelings of mental confusion. It can be very difficult when, as a rescue medium, you have literally to feel the trauma and heartache they went through before they passed over, and why they resisted walking towards the light. Although it may sound a scary prospect it is something we have to do, so we 'invite' the spirits to tell us how they were feeling at the point of death or at a poignant time in their lives in order to tell their story. What we both experienced during our investigation made sense when the story emerged after the research had been collated. Our helper showed us a number of clues and images, which included a church and a cross, so we knew we had a religious theme somewhere within the investigation. All these clues, plus names we were given, would enable us to collate all the information and eventually place that final piece of the jigsaw.

As the two trapped spirits were guided towards us, we could see our helper waiting for them. He beckoned to them and walked them along the path towards a doorway which he opened, and the three of them walked into the light together. We made sure that the door was shut and heaved a sigh of relief.

On the last day of the shoot, which we call the 'Show and Tell', information is at last shared with the homeowners as Jackie and I talk them through our investigation and tell them who the spirits are that have finally been sent to the light. Hurrah! We show the homeowners evidence of the independent research gathered by our head researcher Edna. Edna writes down by hand everything Jackie and I say when walking through the property and during the rescue of the spirit to the light. She will then research this evidence by talking to the local historian and trawling through hundreds of archive records so that we can produce the facts of the haunting to the homeowners.

Our helper during this episode turned out to be a man of the cloth called Father McSpirit. (It was his real name which I thought was amazing.) During the Show and Tell, the homeowners showed us a recent photograph they had taken which quite clearly showed the markings of a large cross in fresh snow just outside their house. The image just appeared and was totally unexplained. This was a religious family who were plagued with the activity of the spirits in their house, and they called the rescue mediums in to help them as they were scared witless. When Jackie and I saw this photograph at the Show and Tell, we truly believed that it was Father McSpirit who had left the mark of the cross in the snow outside their home to let them know that he would help them. It gets better! The shape of the cross that had appeared in the snow was a match made in Heaven. It was a mirror image of the cross that stood on top of the church from which Father McSpirit preached.

"The artist alone sees spirits but after he has told of their appearing to him, everybody sees them."

—JOHANN WOLFGANG VON GOETHE

The day prior to filming, Jackie and I write out our premonitions and our psychic drawing separately (usually in our respective suites in Toronto). The information we receive in order to create this psychic work is given to us by our spirit guides. The type of information we receive from them is in relation to the home we are to visit the following day, therefore having premonitions about what we will find when we get to the property. The list means nothing to us at the time, as we don't know anything about the homeowners, location, or what has occurred in the house that prompted the owners to ask for the rescue mediums' help. This retains the authenticity and honesty of the show, which makes it one of a kind, as both Jackie and I have to do our investigation purely on the information we receive from our spirit guides and our heightened psychic antennae.

Our premonitions are read out to each other on camera during the morning of the investigation. I love this part of the show because although Jackie and I receive separate information, it's uncanny how much we link in to each other. It is evident throughout that our respective guides are linking in with each other as well as with us. It is true spiritual teamwork!

"I have come to believe that there are infinite passageways out of the shadows, infinite vehicles to transport us into the light."

—MARTHA BECK

For those of you who haven't yet seen the show, our producer comes up with an unusual form of arrival for each episode. Neither Jackie nor I are aware of what our arrival at the home will be like – it is all kept under wraps until the actual point of the arrival itself. Both of us love the fact that we know nothing about the arrival, homeowners, activity in the property or the daft joke and venue for our 'Cheers' at the end of the episode. It all adds to the authenticity of the show. For many of you who have watched the show, you will know that our form of arrival can be very unusual, to put it mildly!

Examples of past arrivals have been hitching a ride in an ice cream van, driving a golf buggy, and a ride in a horse box together with bemused horse! One of the creepiest forms of arrival was lying down in a hearse – I remember not wanting to do that one as I felt it was disrespectful, but as usual we both got on with it and it wasn't as bad as I thought. I have to say though I was saying a silent prayer of apology to whoever had lain in the hearse before us!

My favourite form of arrival was where I was a pillion rider on a motor bike whilst Jackie sat in the side car. Sometimes we arrive on foot but there is always a mad twist – it's never straightforward! We have arrived sliding around on snow shoes and we've been 'lost' in a forest, 'walked for miles' up and down winding roads, and 'jumped from the sky' with our umbrellas in Mary Poppins style to name but a few! However, the funniest one for me was when Michael asked us to walk through an alleyway, telling us not to turn around. As the cameras started to roll, we heard a loud clopping noise behind us. Michael reiterated for us not to turn round, but the noise got louder and louder and I remember thinking there was a horse chasing us and as I shouted the warning to Jackie we both started running and screaming at the same time. When the noise seemed directly behind us we turned round to see two transvestites dressed to the nines, resplendent in wigs, lots of make-up and *very* high heels which explained the clopping noise! We fell about laughing as the two guys linked arms with us and Michael shouted, "Cut! I told you not to turn round."

The Cheers is a favourite with fans of the show as they know that both of the rescue mediums are safe and we have once again outsmarted the spirit and done our thing. It is also a relief for me, especially after being on the receiving end of a nasty spirit. In fact I am so grateful for our cheers that I feel like snatching the whole bottle of wine out of Michael's hand and downing it in one!

After the Show and Tell, Jackie and I are given a glass of something, either wine or a soft drink and we have to say a dreadful pun which is written by our producer Michael. As the cameras roll we have to talk briefly about how the rescue has gone, then we say the joke and bang our glasses together saying "Cheers!" The joke has to tie in with what we have found during our investigation and includes the location of the haunting, be it the property or the relevant town. Sometimes Jackie and I add our own puns and the producer loves it as our British quirky humour is a winner with viewers.

There are so many bad puns but sometimes it's not the joke that's funny, it's the reaction of either Jackie or myself and they often keep this in the final cut which is shown at the end of the episode. One such incident was where we were doing our Cheers in a graveyard on a very cold day. Gregory, our director, had given both Jackie and me a hip flask to drink from. He had told us earlier on that it would probably contain cordial. The cameras rolled as I turned to Jackie and said my bit of the joke first. I took a massive swig from the hip flask then proceeded to splutter and gasp as the neat brandy hurtled down my throat. They had changed their mind about the drink as they thought a strong spirit would warm us up but they forgot to tell us! They kept this bit in the show as it looked so funny.

"It takes hands to build a house, but only hearts can build a home."

—ANONYMOUS

Working on the show has been such an amazing experience for me in more ways than one, but I can honestly say that I have met such beautiful people along the way. Our homeowners are ordinary, down-to-earth people who are trying to live their lives in the best way they can, only something has been stopping them in their tracks. They greet us quirky English ladies into their homes and make us feel like old friends.

Our job as rescue mediums is to go to their home and try to find out who is causing such unrest. My heart has gone out to so many people when I can see how such unexplained activity from spirit can affect them and, as everyone is different, the end result can differ from home to home. Some people have been on the verge of having nervous breakdowns, some experienced physical pain, others felt depressed and at their wits' end. What amazes me though is that no matter what they are going through, they make our whole crew feel welcome in their homes. Sometimes there are ten or eleven of us and we completely take over the house for three days. There are often treats left for us such as home-made cookies and in some cases wine, and although we never partake during filming, a nice glass of wine is always welcome after a rescue.

Each and every one of the homeowners that I have met during my time as co-host on Rescue Mediums has been a wonderful, warm and welcoming person and I couldn't have asked for more.

> *"Oh beautiful rainbow all woven of light! There's not in thy tissue one shadow of night; Heaven surely is open when thou dost appear, and bending above thee the angels draw near, and sing The Rainbow, The Rainbow! The smile of God is here."*
>
> —SARAH JOSEPHA HALE

One of my favourite times on Rescue Mediums was my very first show called Over the Rainbow. I felt excited from the very start as Jackie and I were reading our premonitions with the homeowners. They are not allowed to give us any information about what they have been experiencing in the home, but they can say "Yes" or "No" and we could tell by their reaction that we were accurate in our premonitions. I read out a particular name from my premonitions and the little girl who had sat quietly through the filming looked up at her mother and beamed. It turned out to be her name and she smiled at me shyly. She was a sweet little girl around seven years old. As we started to involve her in the conversation we both said afterwards that we felt she was 'a rainbow child'[1]. As we walked around the house we encountered two spirit children but we never saw them together. One was a boy and one was a girl. The little boy showed himself to me holding a bucket and said that he had been catching tadpoles. He was soaking wet through, leaving puddles on the floor. With sudden horror I realised that he was showing me that he had drowned. He continued to communicate with me, and Jackie communi-

---

[1] See the explanation of this in Chapter 6, under Children of the Light.

cated with the girl who turned out to be his sister. He had been searching for her and she had come forward to help guide him towards the light.

It took a lot of patience and planning as the little boy was confused and frightened. We gained his trust and we saw the light coming down and his sister holding her hand out to him. They walked into the light together and at last they were reunited. When Edna had done the research, she found out that the little boy had indeed drowned and that he had a sister called Sadie. When we saw the pictures of Sadie, the resemblance between her and the homeowners' daughter was remarkable. No wonder he was drawn to the little girl as she reminded him of his own sister whom he had been trying to reach for such a long time. After the Show and Tell, as Jackie and I were leaving the house, I happened to look up at the sky and there was the most beautiful rainbow. What a lovely welcome from spirit for me on my first show.

"The night walked down the sky with the moon in her hand."

—FREDERICK L KNOWLES

Without a doubt, this was the scariest show for me. It was at the beginning of 2011, towards the end of our seasons 6 and 7. I knew this was going to be a nasty one because the evening before we started filming I woke up in my suite in Toronto with the feeling of someone lying on top of me, pinning me down on the bed. I screamed out loud and thrashed around trying to move my invisible assailant. The pressure got stronger, I felt a deep and intense cold swirling around me and I couldn't breathe properly. I called out to Archangel Michael to help me and I could visualise him wrapped in a beautiful blue ray of light holding his shield before him. The entity retreated, but I was absolutely petrified. I switched the light on and jumped out of bed going into each room to check that it had definitely gone – I even looked under the bed and in the wardrobes. I kept the light on for the rest of the night wondering what on Earth we were getting into. As dawn approached I knew it wouldn't be long before I found out.

At the 'Meet and Greet', both Jackie and I warmed to the homeowners Leeanne and Willy. They were both welcoming, lovely down-to-earth people but my heart ached for them because as we read our premonitions out to them it was evident there was a very dark presence in the property and Leeane's reaction appeared to confirm our suspicions. What happened on the show still sends shivers down my spine even now. Below is an account I wrote in my journal after we had finished. I hope you are sitting comfortably...

"Leeanne in particular was nodding away as we read our respective premonitions to the couple. What was creepy was that most of her nodding took place when we read out premonitions such as 'A dark foreboding presence', 'Dark shadows that have been seen', 'Feelings of being followed', 'Dark depression', 'Items being moved' and 'Hearing unexplained noises and footsteps on the stairs'. Both Jackie and I glanced at each other and I knew straight away that I was going to experience extremely strong paranormal activity.

"Once the homeowners had left, Jackie and I walked around the property doing our investigation and picking up clues. It was very strange because on the surface there didn't seem to be much activity at all. I remember wondering what was going on because the premonitions and drawings seemed to lead to a very dark place and yet here we were being left 'in the dark', so to speak. However, we both said that we felt there was something bubbling under the surface. How very true this was.

"Both of us felt that we were being watched and it felt extremely unnerving as whoever it was obviously had no intention of showing themselves or communicating with us; we felt as if we were being 'played with'. I remember feeling as if someone had tripped me, nearly causing me to fall down a flight of stairs and maybe this was a clue in itself. Not long afterwards Jackie also tripped up on the stairs. Was this a warning of what was to come?

"On the day of the rescue we 'opened up' our chakras as usual and made sure that we put psychic protection around ourselves. I always imagine wrapping myself in white light and putting on a purple cloak; purple is a spiritual colour and denotes intuition and balance. It's imperative that we prepare for the rescue in this way because if we didn't then there could be very nasty consequences. During the rescue we invite the spirit to come forward so we can find out their story and why they are haunting the property. As we started to fill the house with light we saw a lovely spirit lady who said she was Leeanne's spirit guide who had come to help us. We wondered why she felt it was necessary as our own spirit guides helped us with our spirit rescue work, but as our own respective guides came in very close we knew instantly that something unexpected was about to happen. I felt that we were being used as bait.

"When it started, everything happened so quickly. I was taken completely and utterly by surprise as the dark entity overshadowed me. It started off by crawling all over me and I felt dizzy, sick and absolutely petrified. Jackie's guide had told her to contain the spirit and how to do this, and I could see Leeanne's guide come forward to take the spirit to the light. As I started to regain my composure I realised there was another one. This one was much stronger and felt more evil than the last one as it made a beeline for me. The utter feeling of terror hit me like a ton of bricks and I felt as if I was going to pass out. I tried to control my thoughts as this time it seemed to be in my head taking over, and I remember Jackie shouting at me but I couldn't respond. Just as I thought I couldn't hold on any more, our own guides, Jackie, and Leeanne's guide managed to contain 'it' and it went into the light.

"By this time I was so weak and I must have slipped in and out of consciousness as I don't remember much about what happened next. I can recall the last entity coming forward so fast that it seemed to slip inside my head and I felt the heat of its breath and the feelings of pure evil. It took over my voice box completely so I couldn't speak; I had absolutely no control over my mouth. It was moving and trembling of its own volition but try as I might, I couldn't utter a word. I was trying to call out to Jackie as she was frantically shouting at me to respond in some way but I couldn't. I felt as if it were taking over my mind. I have never been so frightened in my entire life. I had absolutely no control over my body and I ended up on the floor. The evil spirit kept showing me horrendous images of decapitated corpses, hangings, and evil faces that seemed to swirl in and out. Inwardly I called out to my spirit guide and the angels for help and I was shown an image of an angel's wings which helped to calm me down, and it was an image that the entity shied away from. I could feel it starting to back off, so I managed to keep the image in my mind's eye and concentrated on it as Jackie shouted to me not to let it take over. As I retained the image of the angel's wings I felt the entity leave my body with a start and again with the help of Leeane's spirit guide, we sent that one over too. I was a nervous wreck by this time and felt extremely weak but I managed to assist Jackie in filling the rest of the house with light."

At the Show and Tell we shared our findings and independent research with the homeowners. We informed them that in our opinion the haunting had started when Leanne had worked at an inn. She confirmed that a few days after she had started work at the inn the activity in their home had commenced. She also said there was something very creepy about the inn and she never liked the place.

Edna had found information about a prison being near the inn. The inhabitants of this prison were nasty and cruel individuals, some of them murderers and most of them were hung at the prison. We felt that the three entities that overshadowed me had been spirits from this place and that they had followed Leanne home from her work at the inn. Thankfully, with the wonderful help of Leanne's spirit guide as well as mine and Jackie's, we were able to contain them and send them over to the light where no doubt they would have many lessons to learn.

One of my premonitions during this episode was 'Rub a dub dub, three men in a tub'. I had to laugh when we were initially driven to the property and passed a sign in the town saying 'Bath'. Not only that, but we sent three very scary spirits over to the light, and Jackie and I did our Cheers at the end of the episode sitting in a bath (fully clothed, I might add) in the middle of a roundabout. So there we had it, my little rhyme was very significant, although that particular premonition didn't make it onto the show.

"You never find yourself until you find the truth."

—PEARL BAILEY

The events in one particular property were so severe that the homeowners fled their home in the middle of the night. The spirit was a particularly nasty one that had taken a liking to the teenage daughter of the homeowners. So much so that she wanted to live in the basement and shut out all of her family. Her mother described how the girl had completely changed. Usually she was a very sweet-natured and intelligent girl with impeccable manners; however she had turned into someone that her own mother didn't recognise and apparently her language was choice, to put it mildly. The spirit had gradually been taking over the young girl and she was there at its bidding. As Jackie and I started our investigation, we felt a nasty male energy around us.

The house itself was beautiful and should have been full of light but instead there were thousands of flies in each room and the property felt oppressive, dark, gloomy and very, very scary. On the day of the rescue, Jackie and I were grounding and opening up to spirit in our director's car when we heard a click as the car doors locked on their own. There were only the two of us with no-one in sight and we certainly didn't lock the doors. Everyone else was inside the property – all our crew, the director and our producer.

It was pitch black outside and we heard a commotion. Getting used to the darkness, we realised with horror that all the horses from a nearby field had escaped and were running through the gardens of the property. They were quite obviously spooked and how on Earth had they got out of the fenced field? It was then that we realised 'something' was trying to keep us out of the house and it seemed ages before anyone came to look for us! We were shouting at the top of our voices and were quite hoarse when a member of the crew came outside to get a piece of equipment out of the van and heard us shouting and banging on the windows to be let out.

Once we got inside the house, the dark and depressing feeling was getting stronger. This entity was unlike anything I had experienced before and it moved at incredible speed. Sometimes it was in front of us and then it would slither away and end up on the ceiling. It changed shape at will and it turned out to be something called a 'shape shifter'. Shape shifters are a lower form of entity that can change from one shape to another. They don't materialise as a human shape, but they can possess a person especially if that person gives permission for the possession. The energy can change shape at will and is extremely hard to contain as it can move up and down the walls, across the ceiling and, as it isn't contained to the house, it can move around outside the property as well.

We definitely had our work cut out with this and it was another first for me. It was extremely hard to communicate with and to cut a very long story short it took us enormous effort, energy and resourcefulness to be able to contain it. Part of its cunning was to show us extremely scary images to try to manipulate us but we persevered and with the help of our spirit guides we managed to find out the spirit's story. It turned out that some of what was conveyed to us was very sad but he was so full of hatred and guilt that he didn't realise that he was making his own living hell, as well as making life hell for the people living in the house.

Once we persuaded him to face his own truth the story begun to unfold. He showed himself at last in human form and we were able to send him to the light.

"She just moved through me. My God, I felt her. I can smell her. It's her. It's her. Smell my clothes. It's her. She's all over me. It's her. She's on me. It's her. I felt her. It's her. It is. It's... it is... it's my baby. It's my baby. She went through my soul."

—From the film Poltergeist

One of the scariest shows we did in Series 4 that shocked me to the core was poltergeist activity at the Sparta Tea Rooms. As we drew up in a horse and cart, the old tea rooms built in the 1800s looked quaint and both Jackie and I couldn't wait to take a look around the property. We were met at the door by a lovely British couple who had, by their reactions to our premonitions, experienced a lot of very scary unexplained activity in the property. Once the homeowners had left, Jackie and I started our psychic investigation outside the property. As soon as we were in the gardens we felt we were being watched from the house so we went back inside to find out who it was.

As we walked through the basement I screamed as I felt cobwebs all over my face. I could see spiders dangling down off the cobwebs and there were lots of them. It was obvious that the family hadn't been in the basement for a very long time. We nearly stepped on a dead bird which gave us the creeps and it was eerily cold down there. All of a sudden we heard a noise and felt a presence with us. When we heard creaking on the stairs we followed to see if we could find out who it was. Upstairs in the tea room we could feel an entity around us and thought it was male so we asked out loud if we were right. Straight away the lights in the room flickered as if confirming what we had said.

When we approached the second floor of the property we felt another presence on the stairs; this time it was a lady. We could also feel the dark male presence nearby so we knew there were at least two spirits haunting the property, one male and one female. The male presence felt dark and foreboding and we felt that he didn't want us there. I said I felt edgy and we both agreed that he seemed to have a quick temper and was trying to stop us carrying out our psychic investigation. At that point we ask him out loud to show us a sign, to do something. Nothing happened at first, so we started to walk around again when all of a sudden we heard a creaking noise behind us. We both swung round to see a cupboard door opening on its own! Both of us screamed with fright and I was shocked to the core as I had never experienced visual poltergeist activity before. Was it the dark male spirit that had opened the cupboard door? Luckily, our fabulous camera crew were able to film the door opening so the viewers were able to see it on the show. I felt really shaky but we had to carry on with our investigation so we decided to check out the bedrooms. The door of the first bedroom seemed to be stuck, but as we both tried to open it to no avail we decided it must be locked as it wouldn't budge. Just as we were about to give up, we heard a click and the latch of the door lifted and we were able to go into the room. It wasn't locked after all...

Once inside the room I could feel a massive temperature drop and we both felt the dark presence around us again. As the female spirit joined us, Jackie felt ill and sat down on the bed. We talked amongst ourselves discussing what we had experienced so far and both felt that the male and female spirits were connected somehow. I heard the male spirit say something about a 'sick bed' and that he 'needed to find her'. We realised at that point that he was talking about the lady spirit and that it was she who was stuck and not him. Jackie told me to lie on the bed and as I did so I felt the lady spirit around me. I started to feel light-headed as she overshadowed me. I could feel her lying over me and felt my face changing into an old woman's face. I could feel heartfelt pain and grief as she transferred all her emotions onto me. Jackie connected with the male spirit and she asked him to look at the lady on the bed and to call her to him. Eventually we were able to unite them and they walked through to the light together.

I felt extremely drained after this one but I was so happy that they were together at last. Both Jackie and I understood why he was creating such strong activity in the house. He wanted to draw our attention to where we needed to be to help the lady spirit, who turned out to be his wife. He was desperate to get help for her and what better way than to create visible poltergeist activity. At last they were reunited. It was a lovely ending and we were able to restore peace again in the lovely tea rooms at Sparta.

"There is always going to be pain, there is always going to be pleasure. But what is not always going to be there is balance, happiness. That is a personal decision."

—ZEN MASTER RAMMA

In another particular episode, I was overshadowed by a male entity. I couldn't work out at first whether I was with one spirit or two, and between Jackie and me we realised that he had two sides to his nature. One minute I could see a lovely garden and flowers, and the next he was making me feel sick, faint and showing me dark and disturbing images.

Before we started the rescue we took a few 'tools of the trade' with us. We had crystals, candles and a cross. I also held a small angel figurine. We had decided to conduct the rescue in the basement of the house because that was where we had felt the strongest energy. As we started filling the house with light the entity came forward and overshadowed me. One minute he was saying nice things and the next he was spitting and cursing. Both of us felt different types of physical pain such as stabbing, pulling and shaking. We talked about what we were going to do during the rescue. We lit the candles and held a crystal each for protection. Both of us held onto the cross and vowed to stay together as we felt he was trying to separate us.

While we were together we were strong – if he managed to come between us, it would be much more difficult to try to contain him.

When he'd had his fun overshadowing me, he went straight to Jackie and she got up off her chair and started to move away from me. I called to her to sit down as he was trying to separate us. I knew that if we stayed together we were a stronger unit and eventually I got her to sit down.

It was starting to get very difficult as both of us felt weak from being overshadowed but we wouldn't give in and eventually we managed to piece together his story. In his lifetime, he'd been a patient at a mental asylum in the Victorian era. The spirit had two sides to his character, one sweet and gentle and the other absolutely horrific. Both sides were shown to us simultaneously throughout the filming as well as us feeling the pain and heartache of the shocking treatment that he had to endure during his time at the asylum. Even our camera crew could feel the desperation of the spirit as well as the immense negativity in that room. Although both of us were feeling weak from the pain and suffering this entity endured, we finally guided him over to the light. Teamwork!

CHAPTER 5

Ramblings and Thoughts

*"The light is what guides you home, the warmth is what
keeps you there."*

—ELLIE RODRIGUEZ

While working on the show in Canada, Jackie and I were asked to dinner at
our producer Michael's house. On this particular evening we were sharing
our thoughts about and love of pre-Raphaelite art with our head of research Edna who also loves the history and works of art of these gifted and
flamboyant men. As we were chatting away I had a vision of Maria, the lady
who had presented herself to me in my meditation a few years earlier.
Jackie knew who she was, as I had excitedly rung her at the time, but I
explained the story to Edna who was fascinated and I wondered why I kept
seeing Maria in my mind's eye all of a sudden. I dismissed it as I thought it
must be because we were talking about pre-Raphaelite art and, of course,
she had been painted by Dante Rossetti.

Well, here is the answer, from my email to Jackie and Edna later on
that evening, entitled 'OMG is it Ruby?'

"Okay, last email now I promise but I am going to show this to John as
just realised something. See the railings and the flower shapes? I draw them
all the time when I am doodling! They are the exact shape of the petals that
I draw. John only commented on it the other day when I was on the
`phone to the hospital making an appointment. I think she must be one of

my guides and she was trying to tell me all that time ago. You don't think she is Ruby, do you? Especially when you said at dinner tonight that you could see Ruby as a pre-Raphaelite model! She has red hair in the Rossetti painting. Ali xxx"

I would like to share with you some ramblings and thoughts that I've experienced as a rescue medium. The simplest way of doing this is to share copies of emails that I have sent to my husband John before, during or after each investigation. John misses me very much when I am in Canada, but he supports me 100% in what I do as he knows it is my destiny to follow my spiritual path helping others along the way. He has a progressive hearing disorder so he can't hear on the `phone; when I am away I can't ring him to share my day with him so I send him emails to tell him what I am up to and how things have gone.

As you can imagine some of the episodes are scarier than others, but even though I have been scared half to death during spirit rescues, I know without a doubt that my spirit guides are with me every step of the way, as are Jackie's. Not only that, as partners in the show Jackie and I have to trust each other completely because more often than not at least one of us will be overshadowed by a spirit when we are trying to make contact with them. Here's a selection of my notes, thoughts and ramblings during some of our visits.

13 July, 2009

Hi babe,

Was a long day yesterday. Got into the motel-type place we were staying at and couldn't sleep properly. Back to the homeowners' house today where we did an arrival with a horse in a horse box and then did the rescue. The place is very old with grand furniture and stained glass windows with a quaint church across the road. Tomorrow should be our day off, but we have to do the prems and pictures for the next location as no days off in between. On Wed, it's the Show and Tell, the Goodbyes and the Cheers, then straight back to Toronto which is about 3 hours away from here.

We have a party on Monday night at our place with a BBQ on the rooftop, then me and Jackie fly back on the Tuesday. Phew! Good luck at hospital tomorrow, let me know how you get on.

17 July, 2009

Hi babe,

We have been working solidly and I am very tired now. We do the rescue today and I am picking up on the emotions already even before I get there. That's not happened before. Have been getting loads of clues for this one, but nothing at moment makes sense. My drawings are changing constantly. Am shattered and need a rest now.

Love you. A xx

15 June, 2010

Hi,

Love you too. What a day! Yeah, I found my birthday card, how did you do that? I didn't think I had a card from you. Well, we did initial prems at Michael's house which went well, then went for lunch with Greg at The Danforth while the rest of the crew went to the location to interview/film the homeowners. Once Greg got the call, we travelled to location (at a place I can't remember the name of!). And we did the Meet and Greet with the homeowners.

Really strange as they didn't take much of the prems but that may be because a lot of what we got is regarding what we will find at the rescue. We did our walkabout, said how we felt on camera, and any names or info we got from our guides. We felt a man, a woman and at least one child, and quite a few clues on one of my drawings. One of Jackie's and mine link in and two of mine seem to lead on from one to the other. We feel we know where we may be doing the rescue tomorrow due to what we experienced together with the clues we had.

Afterwards we went for dinner with the whole crew to a place called Shoeless Joe's. What a funny name! And unbeknown to me, the waitresses came out singing with an ice cream cake topped with a sparkler for my birthday! Greg and Michael had organised it! I received more cards from Jackie and Edna and some presents. Had a lovely day, but really tired now so going to bed in a bit.

20 June, 2010

I am having more and more prophetic dreams since being here and coincidences for both of us are unbelievable. (Will tell you all about them when I get a chance). Well, the weather here has been hot, hot, hot but not been out in it too much as doing prems and drawings or working filming inside the homeowners' house which is mad hot as we can't have the air conditioning on because it is so noisy. I have been anxious about this one. I will tell you now and we felt (and we were right) that it was a dark demonic one. I feel it will be great when the editors have put it together as some very scary moments. Once I was in the zone though, I just went with what I was being given and what I felt. How we can tell the homeowners everything at the Show and Tell I don't know as there was so much that happened. While we were doing the rescue, we heard footsteps overhead (no-one walking around) and heard knocking on the walls. Even the cameramen and the sound guy heard it. I would say they were the loudest unexplained noises in a property I have ever heard.

I had a dream about Pam the evening before we went to the property for the first time, and the lady in the house is a Pam! And what about this, how weird? We had an electrical blackout the other night and I came out of my room in my lovely pink slippers, got into a lift (yes it was still working!) with a guy who spoke to me in an Aussie accent. I asked him which part of Australia he was from and he said Sydney. I said that my cousin Gillian lived in Perth. The next day, I met the young girl who lived in the house and her name was Sydney! What are the chances of getting in a lift at exactly the same time as a guy from Sydney then meeting a girl in the house the day after with the same name?

We are on location at the next place because the city is in a mess with traffic because of the G20 summit and certain roads are blocked off. Some traffic is already at a standstill, it really is a nightmare. Wonder where we will be going? Another mystery tour! Love you loads. Have your photo here with me. X

7 October, 2010

Hi babe,

Waiting for Edna to pick us up. It is the rescue today. This property is in the city for the first time ever! It's in a place called Cabbage Town. A large old property that is now flats. There is a basement which is outside and one of my psychic drawings is of a large owl. Imagine my surprise when we walked outside on the way to the basement, and there he is, on the fence, a huge owl just like I had drawn!

23 January, 2011

Hi Babe,

It is now 12.40 here! Edna is picking us up at 10.00pm tomorrow, as it is our all-nighter... how scary is that! I will do one or two drawings tomorrow, then will need to go out for some fresh air as I can't stay in here until the evening as it would drive me mad! Although it is arctic-type cold outside, something like 13 degrees minus or something. We think we have it cold... this is something else! I have to wear a massive thick coat, boots, two pairs of socks, hat and gloves and I am still cold! (You would hate it.) Apparently February is worse - as if it could be colder than now!

Have lots to tell you which will be good when I come home. Trying to stay up as late as possible for tomorrow - as working right through the evening so getting into practice! I reckon I will start flagging around 2.30-ish... Will probably get up around 11 a.m. and do a drawing or two, then I will go out just to get some fresh air. Will connect with Jackie around 5.30 p.m. and we will go to get some dinner locally then chill until Edna picks us up. We start filming the initial prems where we read them out to each other at 10.45 p.m. We'll be reading the prems to the homeowners around 1 a.m. How weird, eh? I don't think it is a house. It must be some sort of workplace I feel. Maybe people who are on shift work or some-thing...

27 January, 2011

Hi babe,

I have had to get up after having a bit of sleep. Getting picked up by Edna at 2.45 a.m... We haven't got over the Rescue 'day' which started at 11 p.m. and we got back around 8 a.m. This time we have to do the Arrival at 3 a.m. and we start the Show and Tell with the two pub staff, at 4 a.m. I am so, so tired and my body doesn't know what's hit it. But I can't sleep on cue. Tried to sleep at 8 p.m. but tossed and turned for 2 hours, and I think I have finally had around two to two and a half hours sleep, if that.

I concentrated on you to get to sleep and floated on a cloud from here in Toronto, to our house. I could feel myself coming in through the front door, up the stairs (Libby greeted me!) and into our bedroom so if you thought you felt someone getting into bed with you and stroking your hair, then it was me, doing my astral travel bit!

Will email you or text you in the morning when we have finished and you will be up. Hope you are having sweet dreams with me in them!! A xxx

1 March, 2011

Hi babe,

Feeling so much better now thank goodness as it's horrid being ill when you are working, especially such long hours. I am tired, but that is normal with what we are doing. We did two rescues last night. The first one I was overshadowed and it was really strong, apparently I was screaming and I frightened half the crew. I think Jackie had a job getting him over to the light as I was with him and was shaking and very emotional and screaming. Phew, glad I wasn't on her end of things. The next one that went through Jackie could see so I helped her over with him but he was much gentler. I had drawn what I thought was a toad, and he had owned The Bull public house, so guess I had drawn a bull frog not a toad! Weird, eh?

Think my Dad was helping with the first one as kept seeing trains. We re-alised that earlier, Jackie had got the name Joyce that came from nowhere and I said that's my Mum's name. She said at the time, "Well, I wonder if your Dad is helping with this one?" The trains were an indication of that, definitely.

I opened my fortune cookie and it said, 'You are headed in the right direction. Trust your instincts.' So that is my message I guess, to go with what I am given even though sometimes it seems so mad. Looking forward to seeing you and having a big hug. These three shows have been really tough. Be interesting to see how the editors put it all together. Its Olivia's 5th birthday tomorrow so if you get chance send a message through to Lauren saying happy birthday to Olivia. I sent a card from here which Lauren said she received and I have sent her one of those lovely eCards with a fairy on it which I think she will love. We can have a little tea party on the Thursday after I come home.

Love you.

"Believe in everything you hold dear. Believe in your dreams and know that the worst is now behind you. If you feel you deserve the best from the limitless universal pool of life, trust from deep within your heart that the best is yet to come... Believe..."

—ALISON WYNNE-RYDER

I would like to share with you some extracts from my Journal, starting with an Angelic Reiki course early in July, 2011.

During the first day we received attunements and initiations direct from the angelic kingdom of light. We learned that we are channels for the beautiful pure angelic healing to be transferred to the recipient and that Angelic Reiki gives us support through the ascension process. During one of our sessions I saw a beautiful lady who wore an iridescent gown of white and pale blue. She went round to each of us in turn and put something small and white into each of our hands. At first I thought they were very small crystals, but they were perfectly round. I described her to our teacher Parveen and I said that in the corner of the room I could see a dragon. I really didn't want to say this at first in case the rest of the class thought I was mad but the image wouldn't go away! Parveen told us that the lady I had seen is the ascended master Quan Yin, who is the goddess of compassion and mercy and one of the 'Lords of Karma'. She is of the pearlescent white ray. She developed the eighth chakra, also associated with the pearl.

So the small white objects that Quan Yin had given to us were pearls! Apparently she is often depicted as riding a dragon which is an ancient symbol for wisdom, strength, and divine powers of transformation. Wow doesn't even begin to cover it!

On the second day we did practical sessions of healing on each other and it was truly wonderful. I kept smelling the distinct scent of roses and remember asking Parveen if she was burning rose oil in the oil burner. She said she wasn't but understood why I could smell roses. She said that she would explain later on.

We learned more on the third day about the ascended masters and the information blew my mind. Parveen explained that Lady Nada's symbol is the pink rose; on Atlantis she served as a priestess in the Temple of Love. Imagine how humble I felt in knowing that both Quan Yin and Lady Nada were working with me on my life's path.

I partnered up this morning in the healing session with the only gentleman on the course. I commenced my healing on him but this time we were asked to bring in the energies of the galactic healers of 100% light. Parveen had explained that these beautiful beings of pure light can show themselves to us in any form. They live amongst the stars in the galaxies and although we may not see them, we should be able to feel their powerful energy. I commenced the healing by calling forth my healing angel, who I now know is Leila. I then called on the ascended masters and could see Quan Yin to my right. I could also smell the beautiful scent of roses again, so I knew that Lady Nada was also present.

When I called on the presence of the galactic healers I didn't see or feel anything at first but then all of a sudden I felt a strong shift of energy from my left and took my time turning to see who had joined us. To my utter surprise there was the most beautiful white-winged unicorn shimmering in a bright light, with a golden horn. I questioned this, wondering if it was my imagination, but the unicorn turned its head to look at me. I saw his shocking blue eyes so vivid, wise and pure. He seemed to say, "Yes I really am here and it is not your imagination." He then bowed his head towards me and turned, taking flight and ascending up into the sky. I felt so humble and emotional after experiencing something so beautiful, especially when

Parveen confirmed that it was one of the galactic healers showing himself to me in the form of a beautiful winged horse.

That evening Parveen rang me to ask if I would like to host a show on her radio station called Celestial Radio. We met that week to discuss it in full and I am now a host on the station.

7 July, 2011

This morning I was given the image of a blue bird by my spirit guides. This seemed quite random but I soon forgot all about it because when I got out of bed and went downstairs John suggested that we went out for the day to the Lake District. This seemed like an excellent idea and as we were driving through Coniston past the lake, John pointed it out as being the lake where Donald Campbell died in the late 1960s when taking part in the world water speed record. He then said it was only in 2001 that his boat Bluebird had been recovered. I couldn't believe it!

On the way home, I was reading my book about Angelic Reiki when John had to slow down suddenly in the car and I jerked forward. I looked up at that point to see what caused him to react in that way, to find that the van in front had braked suddenly, and there on the back of the van was a picture of a bluebird! I pointed it out to John and he said that I wouldn't have looked up from my book if he hadn't had to slow down suddenly, so I would have missed that sign. My guides obviously wanted me to see it! Once home, I decided to 'Google' the meaning of the bluebird:

"When the bluebird appears, it brings with it, love, happiness, joy and hope, helping you to look within and embrace the beauty of who you really are. Birds are messengers and the bluebird is no different. It teaches you about admiration and is one of the most admired birds in North America. Just think about how many songs, stories and poems have been written about the bluebird. It is a symbol of love and contentment. The Indians considered the bluebird sacred because its colour is the same as the sky. A beautiful story is that the Cherokee and Pima Indians believed that once upon a time the bluebirds were grey or white, then one day one of the birds found a lake in the mountains. Once it bathed in it, her feathers turned as blue as the sky."

8 July, 2011

John had to go to St. Paul's Eye Hospital in Liverpool this morning and I went with him. As we came out of the hospital I turned on my mobile 'phone and saw an email from the Fairies and Angels magazine, all about a radio show: 11.11, higher consciousness, love, light and oneness. The message also included details of a book called A Guidebook to Angels, Angelic Healing and Angelic Manifesting! My 'phone beeped as another message came through from Chrissie Astell of Angel Light and part of her blog entitled Spirit In The Trees which as the title hints is all about the beauty and power of trees, ensuring that we are grounded as well as embracing mother Earth. As we drove home, we decided to do a detour through Warrington to get some filters from the spa and hot tub shop. They were shut and as they didn't open until 11 we decided to go and get a coffee; as I was sipping mine feeling concerned and a little confused about the outcome of certain things I was aware of a song that came on the radio. My heart leapt as I heard the title Everything's Gonna Be Alright. I looked at my watch for no apparent reason, and saw the time was 11.11...

When we got home there was a knock at the door and the guy from Green Thumb had come to treat our lawns, which is my little part of Mother Earth that I get so much pleasure from; I enjoy sitting in the garden amongst the plants and trees when it's not raining as it is right now. Coincidences? I don't think so.

24 July, 2011

The morning before my Angel Workshop, I had a message on Facebook today from a fan of Rescue Mediums. It was in reply to some information I had offered as assistance with unexplained incidents in her home. This is her message:

"Thank you for answering. You are sweet and it comes out on screen. Please keep those episodes coming. I am hoping to see a book in the future, because so many people are non-believers, until they experience it. Like my husband who finally saw two children running around outside our home during the day, only to realize it couldn't be, because the window is too high, close to 7 ft high, as if they were on a non-existent veranda."

I replied: "Hi, funny you should mention a book! I have had confirmation for some time now from my loved ones in spirit and the angels that I will be writing a book." I then asked if I could quote her message.

"Hello Alison, please don't laugh, I had a dream that the book was in store... LOL. Of course you can include anything you want, it would be my pleasure. I can even send you some photos of orbs taken in my home... I took several at the same time; some have the orbs but right after they are gone into another room. My daughter is quite good at spotting them. They don't bother us, so far... in fact they help us, and they even open a door that is stuck for me.

"My hubby is now a believer, he is into spirituality himself, has been for many years. I am into angels, guides and lots of meditation. My grandchild came over when we bought the house and asked if she could go upstairs to play with the children - she was two and a half at the time. So go ahead, use whatever you like. Take care."

My Angel Workshop was amazing; there were eleven of us in total. We could all feel the presence of Archangel Michael as he came into the room to cut ties to the past, and as one lady said within one of our beautiful meditations: "I was getting so hot," (this is normal when the room is full of angels and spirit guides!) "that I asked if the angels could help me." So that was why the door to the room opened halfway through the meditation and a lovely cool breeze came into the room!

Something funny but usual happened to me on that day. We had just had a well-deserved break mid-afternoon, when I went to invite everyone back into the room. I saw someone sitting on the settee in the main lounge area and I said to them, "Come on, we are ready to start now", turned my back to them and went back into the room only to find everyone already sitting there. I dashed out of the room and of course, there was no-one physical sitting there! So I had more attendees than I thought and whoever it was liked the beautiful energies so much they wanted to join in!

Here is a message from one of the participants:

"I can't even tell you how peaceful I've felt since getting home yesterday. I'm still very much riding my angelic energy high! I can't recommend the course enough. I'm sorting my angel altar this week and I've got a spot cleared, all I need now is to get some new candles and start filling it. Thank you for introducing me to this new and amazing side of spirituality. Angels, where have you been all my life?"

29 July, 2011

I did my first stint with Parveen on Celestial Radio.

When I meditated this morning I asked for Zamil's strength around me. I was dancing with him outside a castle which then changed to a lovely garden, a gate opening and the side of a large building that had pillars on the side of it. I believe this is somewhere I am going to visit. I also had the message that I would go to Montreal. That's a part of Canada I have never been to before.

Just before I went on air I did some deep breathing exercises and had already grounded and put psychic protection around myself. I have been on TV so why am I so nervous about being on the radio? I gave myself a good talking to and told myself to calm down. Parveen, with her lovely gentle voice, opened up the interview and I instantly felt at ease. One of the questions she asked me was, "If a person has lost a loved one, can they contact a medium and what would they get from that?"

My answer was this (a condensed version): "Very often I do get people coming to me when they have lost a loved one. Without breaching client confidentiality, I once had a lady in spirit in the room with me before my client even turned up for their reading! She had been waiting for him and the love that I felt from her was amazing. The energies around her were lovely and as my client sat there she was standing beside me telling me proudly that he was her son. She then proceeded to go over to him and straighten his tie! She went on to give me succinct information that was personal to both of them. I then gave him her name and he couldn't believe it. This was what he was waiting for, as confirmation. I felt blessed to be part of something so beautiful and profound."

7 July, 2011

This was the morning of my hospital admission. I had been questioning a few things that are not balanced in my life so I spoke to the angels before I had to go in for a small operation. My message came through psychic writing.

Understand the flow of your heart with every breath you take. Feel us around you now, as you manifest what is right for you and yours. Do not turn back, as you need to move forward on your new life's path. Those people who helped you turn a corner will be there for you as true beings of light. Do not try to determine the outcome of any situation. Just remain in the here and now... Your time will come and it will be sooner than you think. Write your thoughts down and don't hold back. Whisper your angels' names and they will be by your side in an instant. Do not worry, my child, as there is light at the end of the tunnel. Do not waver or lose the light of love that you carry for others. Be gentle with yourself and believe and trust that we have heard your prayers and are working on a solution that benefits all concerned. Rest assured... Have patience as things are unfolding nicely in the background. We are sending you the blue ray from Archangel Michael and the purest white ray from Archangel Gabriel.

I was then guided to pick three of my Avalon cards and chose:

The Serpent – for knowledge and healing;

The Stag – for pride and leadership;

The Cow – for nourishment, abundance, asking and receiving.

I was then asked to pick another general card from my Angel Cards. It was 'Abundance': "It is time for your life to flow with prosperity, love and success. You draw from the limitless universal pool according to your belief in how much you deserve. Angel wisdom is reminding you now to believe in yourself and trust that you deserve more. Then you will attract abundance and the true riches of life. To feel surrounded by love, open your heart to others. Choose to do what fulfils you most and the angels will bring you joy, satisfaction and success. Enhance your prosperity by receiving graciously, giving out willingly and saying 'Thank you' for everything. Enjoy all you have, and more will come to you. Affirmation: I deserve love, prosperity and success."

I was then dictated the passage that follows, entitled The Angel Within:

Seek the truth in all you do, looking for answers deep within your soul. Ex-

amine that which needs to go and release burdens of the past. Let it be said that enough is enough – you should not have a care in the world. You are entering a new phase in your life, saying goodbye to trouble and strife. Ask your angels so pure and true, to release old patterns so wrong for you. As you become your new best friend, feel the strength and wisdom within. Feel the breath of angels on your cheek and release your cares to the Heavens. Hear the music of your soul as you float on the tide of love.

Zamil then took me on a wonderful meditation. He showed me some doors and asked me to knock on one, which I did. I could see light under the door and it opened into a beautiful garden with a lovely welcoming stream that seemed to glisten in the sunlight. I found myself swimming around in the water with turtles and dolphins. While drying myself by a stream, I could see swans and an angel came out of the water towards me. She said, "Your feathers are wet." I said I didn't have feathers and she said, "You were swimming just now with the dolphins and turtles, were you not?" She then said, "The feathers on your wings are still wet." I could then feel something around my shoulder blades and realised that she had been telling me I had wings! She smiled and told me I was an Earth angel and had work to do. She told me not to worry as the angels would guide me and give me strength. I wondered what she meant by this, but a few months later it all became very clear.

3 August, 2011

I met a lovely lady today who had returned to me for a reading. This morning I did a meditation and received this poem from my spirit guide, the words coming from the lady's husband who is now in spirit. This is what he said:

It is so beautiful here, full of colour, love and peace. I send you blessings, dear, wrapped in a comfort blanket of bliss. I am in pain no more, so no need for worry or stress. I can sing from my soul's very core, sending you a feather from above to caress.

That poem gave her so much comfort; she said that it was the first time she had cried as previously she felt she had to be strong for her family, and this was a release for her. She knew her husband was fine but it was nice to have the confirmation; she is a spiritual lady herself and could feel his presence around her at home. This for me was one of the most beautiful and direct messages from spirit I'd ever received.

2 September, 2011

Tonight I felt quite restless. Eventually, I got comfortable and felt that I was drifting off to sleep. I felt John stroking my face gently, and I thought to myself, "He must have realised that I couldn't get to sleep." I opened my eyes to thank him and heard him give a little snore. I looked over at him and could see he was facing away from me, fast asleep!

4 September, 2011

Last night I had a vivid dream where my Dad (in spirit) was by my side. I knew he was there, but when I tried to remember his face I found that I couldn't see him – I sensed him and knew without a doubt that he had visited me in my dream. He didn't speak, just pointed upwards to a branch where a robin sat. I said, "I love robins." That was it... Seeing a robin in a dream means 'New beginnings and a time for growth – a new lease of life'. Thank you so much, Dad, for this confirmation.

11 October, 2011

My husband John has suffered with a progressive hearing loss which started a number of years ago. He went to see his doctor thinking he had an ear infection only to be told that he was going deaf. He was sent to the local hospital for a national health hearing aid which he never wore. Two years later when he had bright flashes in front of his eyes he was told by a specialist that he had cancer of the brain and would die within five years. After being referred to a different specialist they then told him that he was suffering from a rare condition called Von Hippel Lindau syndrome and he had to travel to Birmingham regularly to have tests done on his eyes. Over the years his hearing got worse and worse, and eventually he had to retire early from the job he absolutely loved as a police sergeant with Cheshire police service.

A couple of years ago, John asked if there was any chance that he could receive his check-up treatment for his eyes at a hospital nearer to where we live, which was agreed. This meant that he didn't have to travel from Cheshire to Birmingham each time. At his appointment last week, John banged his nose on the eye machine and it caused him great pain. He mentioned to the specialist that he had also had a couple of major nose bleeds and the specialist said he would like a different person to run some tests at St Paul's Hospital in Liverpool. Since being a patient at this hospital they have found out that he has a condition called Vasculitis. There are different forms of the disease and the one that John suffers from is called Wegener's Gramulatosis which is quite rare. The specialist at Liverpool said they will try to preserve the hearing he has left, but he has to start chemotherapy treatment which will last for six months but will hopefully keep the condition at bay. It was explained to us that it is a serious disease and that John will be poorly with the chemotherapy, but he has to go through it if it helps in the long term.

At present I feel extremely angry that John has been misdiagnosed for all these years, and if he had been diagnosed properly then his hearing could have been saved. I am trying to be brave in front of John but inside I have been crying out for help. I have called on the angels more times than I can remember these last few days and today has been no exception. How I would have got through this pain without their help doesn't even bear thinking about. It also brought home to me that I have drastic decisions to make and the first one was that it was time for me to leave Feathers. My spirit guides and the angels have been giving me messages about moving on and new beginnings. Sometimes we have to just take the bull by the horns and stop resisting the flow of life. I have enjoyed my time there for a number of years but things happen for a reason and it was now time for me to leave. My heart was telling me that I was doing the right thing and I know now that I have to fly the nest and soar.

I know that the angels have been wrapping me in their healing wings, and that my Dad appeared in my dream to help prepare me for the inevitable. My husband is very poorly and I have to take care of him. Everything else will have to go on the backburner. I know I can do this with the help of my loved ones in spirit, the angels and my spirit guides.

Even though I know that things will remain steady for a while and I have to be at home to look after John, the angels continue to give me messages through inspirational writing. I know what they say is true, that new ventures will come my way and their words fill me with love, gratitude and excitement:

There is nothing more that you can do at this present time. Everything is unfolding nicely so have patience. You will soon find out what exciting ventures we have in store for you. Just believe and trust in us. Make way for new opportunities that will open up, as you meet new acquaintances. There will be surprises around the corner, and a new sense of relief and calm will surround you. Wish upon a star for clarity of your dreams and don't hold back. Those who wait reap rewards and this is a time of transformation in the best possible sense.

I have decided to heed their advice and go with the flow. I don't have to do anything as they are taking care of everything. I am trying my hardest not to worry about John as he is my life, but I have faith and trust in the unconditional love of the angels. I am tired now and know that this is a time for rest and rejuvenation.

It's interesting as people come to me with their problems and I do everything I can to help them and to see things in a more positive way. I give them wonderful messages and confirmation from spirit in readings; but for myself, I can't always see the wood for the trees. Speak to any other medium or healer and they will often tell you the same. People don't always realise that we too have doubts, we too have worries and concerns, and we also feel down at times. However the difference is that we can speak to our spirit guides or the angels, tell them what is concerning us and know how to hear or be able to decipher their wonderful messages and guidance.

11 October, 2011

I wrote to a couple of magazines asking if they would like me to do a regular column for them or a one-off feature. I heard back from Prediction magazine's editor Alexandra, who said she would be happy to discuss future projects with me. I have a Skype meeting with her on the 31st October when I am in Spain. How apt – Hallowe'en... After receiving the message I did a meditation and turned over a couple of angel cards.

'Synchronicity': "Rejoice when you notice coincidences and synchronicity as they are carefully orchestrated events from the hand of spirit. They are the angels' messages to you that you are on the right path. Start to expect them and look for them. Be aware that there is a divine reason behind them, and consider what the message or lesson is. Synchronicity is also a reminder to you that all things happen in divine timing. Affirmation: All things happen in perfect timing."

I then turned over the 'Power' card: "The angels are helping me to regain my power and stand on my own two feet, not letting others take my energy or power. I am moving forward with confidence, knowing I am on the right path." As I finished my meditation, Zamil handed me a leaf. When I looked this up, it means 'To prosper'. Thank you, dear angels, thank you... I feel much stronger and more positive now.

25 October, 2011

John has to start chemotherapy soon and we have been warned how poorly he may become whilst on the treatment as he has to take a large dose of steroids at the same time. We have decided to fly out to our place in Spain on an impromptu holiday. We both need the break and to get away from everything and, in some respects, everybody. As soon as we arrived at our apartment we both heaved a sigh of relief – a bit of sun in a different environment is going to be great and this will be the last holiday that John will be able to have for over six months as the hospital have told him he can't fly whilst on his treatment. We are going to enjoy this holiday relaxing on the beach and catching up with friends Kevin and Michelle who live near our apartment. They always cheer us up as Michelle is so funny; we both need to laugh until our sides ache. We are going to enjoy this holiday!

27 October, 2011

John and I went for a walk along the beach at Guardamar and I inwardly asked my angels to give me a sign of a feather that everything would be fine. Straight away, my mind was saying, "Don't be silly, how can they do that, this is a beach!" However, in my heart, I knew they wouldn't let me down. We walked a long way along the beach feeling the heat of the sun on our faces and hearing the waves crashing on the sand. There really is nothing like being by the sea to rejuvenate one's soul. As we started walking back the way we had come, we were about half-way there and I just happened to look down. There, lying on the sand was a very large and soggy white feather. I smiled as I dried it, shared my wonderful experience with John, and put it in my bag. It now has pride of place on the sideboard in our apartment. Thank you, angels.

31 October, 2011

Hallowe'en, in Spain! I had a Skype meeting today with Alex, the editor of Prediction magazine. Our meeting went well as Alex is such a lovely vibrant soul. I pitched a few ideas to her and she said she'll get back to me. I have already written a piece about my take on, and predictions for, the year 2012 for their New Year Special Edition which will be in the shops in December.

15 November, 2011

I watched myself on the ITV show May the Best House Win. I haven't laughed so much for ages. Laughter really is the best policy, and the angels love fun people. That is why angels fly, as they take themselves lightly! Everyone has been sending me positive feedback on Facebook and I was getting texts all day from friends who had watched and enjoyed the show.

16 November, 2011

John and I went to the hospital today and he had his brain scan. I imagined him in there wrapped in a beautiful white light and asked the angels to be with him.

17 November, 2011

I went to the Antique Centre at the bottom of our hill to take some of my Dad's items that Mum wanted to sell and they are now going to auction.

Whilst there I was speaking to two people who work there. They said I could work there doing readings on the run-up to Christmas as they will be having a few evenings where they stay open until 7.30 p.m. Two of them are also going to have tables at my Christmas Fair.

19 November, 2011

John was out at his friend's house today so I had an 'angel day' all to myself. I did my cards and meditated in my room at the bottom of the garden. Whilst in there, I asked out loud if I could see an angel. I had done an angel spell a few minutes earlier and the white candle I used for the spell was still lit. As I gazed at the candle flame, the flame rose and it turned into the distinct shape of an angel. I could see the head, the wings and the gown. I blinked and looked again, but the angel was there as clear as anything within the flame. I felt so honoured and such a deep and wonderful peace. Thank you, angels.

Christmas came and went but I didn't feel like celebrating as John was so ill and I hated seeing him like this. However, we put on a brave face for the family as it was tradition that they come to us for Christmas lunch and everyone opens their presents together. John was so ill that he couldn't eat his Christmas lunch although he was wonderful with the children. He gets very weary as well as being sick, so he had to go to bed in the end and it wasn't the best Christmas ever. I made sure that the girls were distracted so they didn't see Granddad being ill as it would have upset them, but they enjoyed opening their presents and we played a few of their new DVDs. In between playing hostess to the family I kept checking on John but after everyone had gone I asked the angels to make him better as it didn't seem fair that someone who had always been there for everyone was not only losing his hearing, but was feeling so weak and helpless and it was breaking my heart. He is such a caring man; he was a policeman for twenty-seven years and has won medals for bravery when he saved two people's lives. I am trying to be strong for both of us but the steroids are making him into someone I don't recognise and to be honest I feel like running away sometimes. I have told no-one this.

23 January, 2012

John is still very poorly on the chemotherapy and is struggling with the steroids so one minute he is being sick with the chemotherapy and on the other hand the steroids are making him sweat and become Mr Angry. I must admit I am struggling at present and it's only my faith in my guides and the angels that are keeping me sane right now. My friends have been wonderful, so supportive, but I don't want to bother them every time I feel down. So I decided to do something about it and joined a choir. I have always loved singing and read somewhere that it is a stress-reliever, so I will try anything!

10 – 11 March, 2012

This weekend I worked at Walton Hall in Warrington doing readings at a Mind, Body and Spirit fair. The venue is an old Victorian mansion with positive energies emanating from each room. It was resplendent with glittery chandeliers, old pictures adorning the walls and a grand old sweeping staircase that I could imagine walking down in a crinoline dress. Okay, I am getting a bit carried away now! I was extremely busy on both days and during each evening I was involved in the psychic night where I did some platform work in front of an audience. What they didn't know was that I had never done platform work before, but as always spirit never let me down and I was amazed at how much information they gave me. People were coming up at the end of the evening to thank me for such succinct information from their loved ones in spirit and I felt so blessed to be able to pass those wonderful messages on.

16 March, 2012

Today I went to Liverpool to the top of the tower to do psychic readings on air for Radio City, with Clare Divine. The show was really successful and we had a lot of people ringing in for their readings with excellent feedback.

31 March – 1 April, 2012

I did readings this weekend at the Nantwich Mind, Body and Spirit fair and I was very busy on both days. My table was right next to someone selling everything angelic from figurines to crystals and pictures. Even though each day was noisy with a lot going on, the ambience of the room felt just right and once I started the readings and was 'in the zone', I didn't even notice how noisy it was!

15 April, 2012

Today was my second Angel Workshop. It was a truly amazing day full of angelic energies and those attending were pure Earth angels. When I asked Archangel Michael to come into the room with his legions of light, we could all feel the energy in the room shifting and creating a euphoric vibration of energy. It was so beautiful.

21 April, 2012

Today my friend brought her little girl to meet me. I knew from what her mother said that she was very spiritual and could talk to spirit and feel them around her but I didn't realise quite how much until I talked to her about her experiences. Some of the things she saw or felt were frightening to her, but when she asked me about a wolf that she kept seeing, I knew that he was her power animal. When I explained all about power animals she said that it made sense because he always appeared when spirit frightened her.

I went through grounding and psychic protection with her, and discussed one spirit that had scared her. She said he was dressed like a farmer and in one incident she could see a horse in agony as if it had been shot. She kept seeing this over and over, as if it were a record stuck on a turntable and I explained that spirit had told me that her wolf would help the horse and that the man himself was frightened and he needed help to go to the light. He was drawn to her because of the psychic light she shone out to the spirit world and he came to her for assistance. (Please refer to Chapter 6 under 'Children of the Light' to read more of Gemma's story and how I helped her.)

26 April, 2012

Tonight I did a two-hour show on Afterlife Talk Radio. My talk was about spirituality in general and I included a beautiful meditation I had written about 'How to meet your guardian angel'. The show was very well received and the producer was happy with the content.

30 April, 2012

Because of John's illness he can't work, and although I am doing readings and healing for people we need a regular wage coming in. I saw a job advertised last week working as a receptionist in a chiropractic clinic. It said it was for two days a week but they wanted flexibility to cover for holidays. I applied and I had my interview today. When I walked into the clinic everything about the place felt right. The feelings I had were good and I felt that I would get the job. My interview went really well and when I came out I felt happy and put my trust in spirit that I would be successful.

10 May, 2012

For the past few weeks I have been taking weekly spiritual classes at home. There are six people who come along. I have called the classes 'Soul Magic' and they are proving very popular. I choose a different theme each week and we always have a lovely group meditation at the beginning of each class.

11 May, 2012

As a medium it's very rare that I have a clairvoyant reading myself but tonight I decided to seek confirmation from the messages I had been receiving from spirit. One of the main things that came out of the reading was that I would be doing more platform work. I was also given a big 'kick up the bum' when the medium asked me, "When are you going to finish your book? It should be out there already, it's going to be successful and you and your book are going to America!" My Dad and Grandma in spirit had messages for me and John's Mum Mary came through as well.

10 June, 2012

I was looking after Olivia today (my six-year old granddaughter) and she stopped to look at my angel picture hanging in the hall. I told her that it was Cupid and she said that she had seen a real angel. I asked her what she meant, and she explained that in their bathroom at home there is a little mirror, and if it's a sunny day the water in the bath reflects and it makes a rainbow that appears in the mirror. Olivia said that she saw her Grandma (my ex-mother-in-law) who died last year. She said she often sees her Grandma 'in the rainbow' and told me that when the rainbow gets brighter, that is when the face appears. Apparently her Grandma doesn't talk to her but she looks like she is trying to, as "Her mouth is moving but there is no sound." Olivia then said, "I think she talks to me in my brain (as she pointed to her brow chakra, the third eye). I know what she is telling me even though I can't hear her – I think that my Grandma is an angel now."

15 June, 2012

Tonight I did my first 'Platform Party'. So what is that when it's at home, I can hear you ask? Well, it's when a group of people get together in some-one's home and I ask their loved ones in spirit to come forward with messag-es. It is very similar to platform work at a psychic event, but on a much smaller and more informal level. During this particular evening there were ten ladies present and I started off the evening by doing mini card readings for them. It didn't take long before spirit started coming through with wonderful information for those present. We had a raffle of a free reading with me and I finished off the evening by doing a questions-and-answers session. Everyone present said how much they enjoyed themselves.

When I asked how they had heard about me, one of the ladies said she had been in the audience at a psychic night at Walton Hall and how much she enjoyed what I had done. She said I had received information for her and her family that no-one else knew and it was confirmation for them that their loved ones in spirit are fine and are around them in a protective way. It was a very successful evening and I gave thanks to the spirit world and my angels.

26 June, 2012

I have to go to work for a meeting later this morning but I am enjoying sitting in the sun on my swing in the garden. I love listening to the birds singing and the rustle of the breeze through the bamboo tree. A robin has just swooped down and landed on my angel statue and he sat looking at me for a while before flying off.

I am writing this only a few hours after having to take my little dog Jet to the vet. A couple of evenings ago I saw a misty image moving on the rug and realised it was my cat Topsy who passed over to the animal spirit world a few years ago. I felt that she was letting me know it was Jet's time and I mentioned this to my husband John. Jet started to go off her food and this morning she struggled to walk, so I rang the vet who told me to take her in this afternoon. During the morning she wouldn't eat her breakfast but I gave her some toast which she ate a little of. Normally our Labrador Libby would have been pouncing all over the place as she would have also wanted some, but she remained sitting down about a yard away from Jet as if to give her some space. Just before we were ready to leave, I went to switch the light on in the bathroom and the light bulb blew. I knew in that instant that we wouldn't be bringing Jet back home – it was spirit's way of preparing me for the inevitable and letting me know that her light in this world would be going out.

When we got to the vet it was an empty clinic; I feel the vet also knew that it was Jet's last day on Earth. We saw a lovely lady vet from America and she laid it on the line for us. Jet was extremely poorly. I had thought she was seventeen (she was a rescue dog) but they had her down as being twenty. All in all she was an old lady and in a lot of discomfort. Apparently she had a very infected womb and also had tumours in her body. The vet suspected cancer but couldn't be sure unless she operated, but even then they were not sure if Jet would pull through. We had a decision to make. Either we could put her through an operation that she may not survive, or we put her out of her misery and let her go without the discomfort of a serious operation. We decided on the latter.

We stayed with her throughout with me stroking her head. She knew I was there, but it was one of the hardest decisions I have ever made and both John and I were distraught. Back at home there was an empty hole and neither of us knew what to do with ourselves and of course there were constant reminders of Jet: her bed, her dish, toys, etcetera. But the guilt was the worst – had we made the right decision? I went to sit on the swing in the garden which is my favourite place and my white cat Celestial (Celeste for short) came straight away to sit on my knee and I felt she was comforting me. Libby came and rested her head on me and my other cat Tara was nearby. Animals know instinctively when someone isn't well and I feel they had known this about Jet for some time now. They were letting me know that I had done the right thing. I had expected Libby to be pining for Jet but she seemed happy and content.

Sitting in the conservatory, John and I were comforting each other, I looked out of the window at the garden. Instantly I saw the image of Jet's head as clear as a bell as if it was suspended over the wisteria at the top of the trellis and I saw her as she was when she was younger, as if looking around. I turned to look behind me in case I had seen the reflection of my other dog Libby, although in my heart I knew I hadn't. Hearing Libby moving around upstairs proved it but of course when I looked back out of the window the vision had gone. However, I knew that without a doubt the angels had given me a vision of my lovely little dog to let me know she had made her final journey to the Rainbow Bridge.

CHAPTER 6

An ABC of Spirituality

A is for Afterlife

"I have always imagined that paradise will be a kind of library."

—J K ROWLING

Many people want to know what the afterlife is like but the truth is you will never know until you pass on from this world to the next. There are many books on the subject and I have just finished one entitled Heaven is for Real, which is the account of the four-year old son of a local pastor and his wife in America. The little boy suffered with a burst appendix and after coming round from his operation he mentioned that he had met Jesus in Heaven. He went into great detail of what he experienced much to the amazement of his family. The book has been written by his father and it really does give one pause for thought.

People have differing views about the afterlife and I am no expert. A spirit hasn't told me per se what it's like on the other side, and I don't believe that anyone on Earth would know for sure until they themselves pass over; when they do, it is my belief that each person has their own unique journey. Through my inspirational writing I have written poems dictated to me by the spirit world which denotes how happy loved ones are in their final resting place. This information generally comes through either before a client comes to see me or when they are having their reading. Their loved ones will do this as they want to reassure those dear to them on Earth that they are free from pain or worry and in a peaceful environment. I have noticed a common theme from spirits who want to convey they are in a better place as they show me beautiful bright colours like nothing we see on Earth, as well as beautiful rainbows, colourful butterflies, a beautiful landscape and an indescribable feeling of love and serenity. I feel this is because in the spirit world souls are free and don't carry the burdens of a human body and mind such as hate, anger, stress or an inability to forgive. A poem that was recently dictated to me was called Remember Me As I Was, and although it wasn't for one particular person, I believe that I had to pass this on to anyone who had lost a loved one who had been in pain before they passed over. The poem was confirmation that their loved one in the spirit world was now at peace, in no more pain, and wanted those here on Earth to remember them in their prime, as well as keep the wonderful memories that they shared together.

No-one will ever know until they pass over themselves if everyone sees the same things, or if it is an individual thing. One of the loveliest and most heartrending films I have ever seen is What Dreams May Come starring Robin Williams. It reduces me to tears every time I watch it. I don't want to tell you too much about it in case you want to watch it yourself, but when Robin's character dies he goes to Heaven and sees a lot of colour in a comforting way. For example he 'sees' purple trees exactly as his wife (an artist) had portrayed them. He also sees a lot of deep green grass, rolling hills and exotic coloured birds and meets up with loved ones as well as his pet dog. There is also an amazing scene where he visits the halls of knowledge, which is a vast expanse full of millions of books and spirits floating around.

I feel that when people die they will often see (especially initially) what was personal and loving to them on Earth. However, it is also my belief (which we have had confirmation of so many times on Rescue Mediums from spirits we have shown over to the light) that there are different 'layers' within the spirit world. Some people will go straight to Heaven whereas others, who had lessons to learn, will be sent to a lower layer of the spirit world. In the film you can see a portrayal of two of the very different layers within the spirit world - Heaven being one, all bright, colourful and peaceful and the lower vibration being dark, foreboding and utter turmoil. Again, it is a very interesting theory as some people believe this is what everyone sees as they pass over, while others believe it could be indicative of that person's mind at the time of passing.

A is also for Angels

"Angel wings surround me, powerful and full of love. I can be anything I want to be, with divine help from above."

—ALISON WYNNE-RYDER

I love working with angelic energy and sharing my knowledge with others either through my angel workshops or over the airwaves on radio. I have shared some of my own experiences of angels through my diary entries and I thought I would include a little more about the celestial realms including real-life stories from friends and relatives.

Angel magic

The following is my own account of creating my angel altar which was one of the wonderful angelic spells and rituals I performed when doing my Angel Magic course which is run by the BSY, who are the UK's number one complementary therapy college. I was so proud when I received my certificate as it meant I could now share the love of the angels with others and help to bring a sprinkling of magic into their lives. Angel magic is about working with the angels to improve your life, and how to bring their beautiful positive and magical essence into your world.

The angels really can help you to get the most out of life and miracles can happen! So let's start with bringing some angel magic into your home. I did, and our home is now brimming with positivity, love and light.

An angel altar is something that has been used since Neolithic times. Nowadays it is a wonderful way of bringing love and light into the home. Houses retain residual energy whether positive or negative and by creating an angel altar you will be inviting the angels to bring spiritual enrichment into your life. We humans tend to hold on to things from the past sometimes for sentimental reasons, even though the items could be from a relationship that is well in the past! These items serve no purpose now and you will be surprised at how positive you start to feel if you do some decluttering. The truth is that all they are doing is gathering dust - just because you shut the door on your clutter doesn't mean that it goes away and the same can be said about your mind. Release any blockages by letting go of resistance and give your worries up to the angels by creating your very own angel altar.

The first thing to do is to choose where you would like your altar to be. It should be a permanent one and it should be on a sturdy piece of furniture, a shelf, mantelpiece or windowsill. My own is on a shelf in our conservatory as it is one of the quietest rooms in the house overlooking the garden and it has a lovely bright and open feel to it. The room feels tranquil and calm so it is a perfect place for me to talk to my angels and meditate. Once you have chosen the area for your altar, ensure that it is clean and free of dust so you can bless your altar by dabbing some essential oil on each corner prior to adding two white candles for purity, truth and wisdom. You don't have to buy items for your altar especially as there will be little treasures around your house that will be a perfect addition. At present on my own altar I have two white candles, a large angel figurine, a gold star, two white feathers, two cleansed crystals and an angel scroll. You can include anything you wish that is of an angelic theme.

In order to charge each item with your energies and love, light the candles on your altar and hold the object in your left hand, cupping your right hand over it. When you are relaxed imagine a golden light around the object and you should feel it becoming warm in your hand. Place it onto your angel altar and do this for each item in turn.

It is important to dedicate your altar to the angels by lighting an incense stick and saying the following:

I dedicate my altar to the celestial realms and ask that the angels enter my life and lovingly guide me. My altar is a link between myself and the angels. So mote it be.

You now have a working altar where you can talk to the angels! Remember that the angelic realms can communicate with you through thought patterns and often share divine guidance through ideas that seem to pop into your head. Know that you can talk to the angels about anything. It will be like talking to an old trusted friend who will listen and not judge. If you are upset or worried, ask them to carry your cares away. If you want help with future ventures, ask them to show you the light; more than anything, remember to say 'Thank you' and believe in their love and guidance.

Guardian Angels

Everyone has a guardian angel who is with them from birth. They help by guiding us and giving us their divine assistance in many ways such as leaving signs of their presence around us. As they are beings of light, they don't experience any of the human emotions that we encounter during our lives on Earth such as anger, hurt, jealousy and hatred. They know only compassion and love. Our guardian angels are with us when it is time for us to depart from Earth and guide us over to the afterlife. I have given my accounts of knowing my angel is around me earlier on in this book but I thought it would be lovely to share with you some true stories from family friends and acquaintances. The following are in answer to a request I put out on Facebook asking people for stories about angels for inclusion in my book. Here are a few of them.

Jasmin

I remember being locked outside a resort some time ago in the middle of a silent highway at the dead of night. It wasn't a fully-fledged tropic resort with good security and, to cut a long story short, earlier that day I heard first-hand that females were in danger if they were outside the resort. Needless to say, I was very afraid and after about an hour of solid crying and trying to shake the gate open something told me to pray, so I did. I asked the divine creator and the archangels to help me get inside.

Moments later a lovely quiet couple emerged from the darkness; I could see them approaching from the light of a street lamp. I was sitting on the ground and as they got nearer I waved to them and when they asked if I was alright I told them that I was locked out. They told me not to worry and that everything would be fine, telling me they were guests at the resort. They had a key to let me in and as the gate opened I thanked them profusely. I ran a few feet, turned around, and they were gone.

Carol

My daughter failed a test at school so she was given a chance to do a rewrite, but to pass she had to bring the test in the next day. She sometimes forgets things so I reminded her how important it was to bring it home that morning. When she got home, I asked if she remembered and she confirmed that she had and thanked me for calling the school to remind her. I told her I hadn't rung the school and she said, "Sure you did, the Secretary called me to the office and told me my Mom had called to remind me to bring home the test." It wasn't me, and I hadn't told ANYONE about it, so we still don't know who made that call!

Meeting the archangels

My son sees spirit. He is seven years old and one night before bed he asked me to put a bubble of protection around him to protect him from the 'ghosts', so I did. About ten minutes later he asked me to do it again. I said I already had, so he looked out of the corner of his eye and pointed to a corner in the room and said, "Who's that?" The first name that popped into my mind was Archangel Michael so this is what I told him. He pointed to another corner in the room and said, "Who's that?" Ariel came to mind so I told him and this went on with him pointing to each corner in the room and me answering with the first archangel's name that came to mind. Finally satisfied, he jumped into bed and fell right to sleep. In the morning he told me that he really liked that "Michael guy" 'cause he looked really tough and had a cool sword! I hadn't described what any of the archangels looked like – he saw that all on his own!

Pam

While Pete and I were in South Africa we hired a car to travel to our next destination. It was a scary ordeal, getting lost, bad weather, bad road conditions. We were driving through moors in the dark, not knowing if we were going to get there and we both prayed to our angels to guide and protect us on our journey. Not long after, we came across a petrol station where a man said he would help to direct us and asked us to follow him for 180 km. He told us that we had been protected by angels and both of us knew that he had been sent to us from the angelic realms to protect us on our car journey.

Layke

I got an angel number in my dream. I was flying in a `plane through a jungle, along a river, very low. We landed and upon getting out I asked the pilot, "What speed does the `plane need to be at in order to take off?" He tells me "241". It's a number I frequently see. Then I woke up. My angel numbers book was beside me on the dresser. It means 'Your connection to the angels is opening your heart to the powerfully healing energy of love. Keep talking to the angels, as they are blessing you and your life.'

Then I called about a job and got it.

Judy

Good morning Alison! So many times you have told us that our angels are there to help us, we just need to ask. Last night my seventeen-year old dog was in great distress; for hours she was panting (which she only does when in pain) and pacing. I tried petting her and massaging her, but I couldn't get her to settle. Thirty minutes after giving her some medication with no change I was becoming very afraid that I was losing her, and then I heard your voice telling me my angels are there for me, I just need to ask for their help. I asked for everyone to help her get through this and to take the pain away in order for her to heal. I kept asking over and over. Fifteen minutes later she was asleep, resting peacefully. I believe it was a combination of the medication and the angels answering my prayers. Today she has gone for a walk, chased a squirrel and jumped up on the porch without using the stairs. Now she's asking for breakfast. Thank you angels!

Caroline

About three years ago I had a hysterectomy and had to have both ovaries removed. I was told at the time I had ovarian cancer so the week before my operation I went to the grotto in Mellorey and prayed to Our Lady asking

Arrival in a hearse

The Rescue Mediums

Arrival with new friends

The Rescue Mediums crew

Cheers!

Ruby

for a sign of hope. On the day of my operation a lady in England who sees angels passed on a message to me through my brother's partner to tell me that I was going to be alright. At the time I was a bit sceptical and thought to myself that time would tell. Imagine my delight when I went back to the hospital for my results and the doctor told me I was borderline and didn't have to receive any more treatments, just check-ups for five years. I only have two more visits to hospital and I thank God I will be finished soon. I know I am a very lucky girl.

Me!

Last week I did a reading for a lady who said she wasn't sure whether she believed in signs from the angels. When I had finished her reading, she stood up and by her feet was a beautiful pure white feather. I rest my case lol! Thank you angels... x

The following true story has to be the best account of the archangels stepping in when we are in danger. When I had finished reading it, I had tears in my eyes, and tingles down my spine.

Bonni

When our family lived in the country for seven years I acquired my school bus license and drove daily a 52 kilometre route in and out of three schools, twice a day. After five years I was ready for something quieter and when I hinted at 'retiring' the owner of the company presented me with a change I couldn't refuse. He needed someone to drive seniors and physically and developmentally challenged adults to a day program designed to keep them social and involved in life and give their caregivers some free time.

I loved my new assignment even though the little bus with the wheelchair lift wasn't always reliable. I daily invoked my angels to see us through our Canadian snow storms, calm my Alzheimer clients and keep us all safe as I wound through three communities to gather my eight riders. My constant co-pilot was Archangel Michael, who oversees travel and safe passage. I envisioned him in his robes of purple and gold sitting with the rest of the crew behind me.

I nicknamed my little bus Jitterbug as she had more than a few quirks that would cause her to shimmy along the road. She was noisy to say the least but, like most bus drivers, I came to know her sounds and listened carefully for changes as I drove. Jitterbug had been making a few clunking noises and creaking more than usual, so for three weeks I had been asking my boss to check her over. His response was always, "She's an old bus, her wheelchair lift is just in need of some oil and rattles around as you drive. She's fine!" I had my doubts, but was under the assumption that he was the expert.

Our son was returning home from two years abroad and had asked me to check out a few car lots, and because it would save me close to an hour on the road I asked permission from the boss to scoot to the next town and walk through a few car lots to price some cars. Something urged me to stay off the major highway and choose to stay on the quiet service road that runs between a nearby nuclear plant and our larger Highway 401. All my seniors had been safely delivered to their day program and I was on my way to the car dealerships. While going through a curve in the road I noticed the rear corner of Jitterbug making some ungodly noises and then all heck broke loose! She veered and jerked and instinctively I wrapped my arms around the wheel and fought to keep the swerving little bus on the road. She came to a stop on the shoulder of the road and I briefly laid my forehead on the wheel between my gripped fists and said a prayer of thanks because I knew whatever happened was big. I thanked God that my charges were safely enjoying their morning tea at the Center.

But it wasn't over just yet. I looked to my right through the tall glass panes at my bus steps and saw my rear wheels rolling by! The axle of the bus was ground into the soft shoulder of the road but the wheels flew as if they had no intention of stopping. I watched helplessly as they gained momentum and bounced a little higher after each time they connected with the road. They shot straight ahead of me and it was then that I noticed the van coming out of the driveway and turning right to drive towards me. He was quite far away but I am sure I could see his eyes widen as he registered the event that was about to transpire. The wheels kept up with their bouncing roll and I prayed, "No, no, God, please help." It wasn't an eloquent or drawn-out prayer full of pleading requests. This was clearly out of my hands. My shoulders and chest ached from the effort it took to control the bus as she came to a stop and I looked down the road ahead of me as I prayed. One of the wheels slowed, then wobbled and flopped harmlessly on its side in the ditch. "Thank you, angels." The second one kept on its path towards the van and I saw the man wrap his arms around his head and duck below the dashboard and steering wheel. He hadn't had time to get out of the way of the unpredictable wheels. It took one more bounce towards his windshield and then the most amazing thing happened. No more than ten feet from connecting, it took a perfect 45 degree turn to the left and disappeared into the ditch as if a giant hand had come down and given it a tap and said, "No, not here… HERE… in the ditch you go!"

A few seconds later I saw the man jump out of the van and run full steam towards me in my wrecked bus. I dropped out of the driver's door of the bus and without exchanging words we hugged. He asked me over and over if I was okay and finally said, "Good Lord! I don't know how you managed to keep this thing from flipping over! You were all over the road." He `phoned the administration office (who in turn called the Ministry of Transportation) and I called my boss. I believe my words were, "I think I know why the bus was making strange noises." I gave him my location and told him to bring a tow truck.

When I turned round my new friend Paul (we had exchanged names between hugs) was climbing around inside the bus. I asked him what he was looking for and he said, "Where's that guy?"

"What other guy?" I asked, "I'm alone."

He laughed and smiled and said, "No. While you were bringing this bus to a halt, I saw a man, a big man bent over behind your seat and his arms were encircling yours. He was helping you to keep control of the bus." I almost fainted when he uttered the next words as I instantly knew who he had seen. "He was huge and was wearing a big puffy purple ski jacket." Thank you, Archangel Michael!

B is for Believe

"It's what you choose to believe that makes you the person you are."

—KAREN MARIE MONING

'Believe' is my mantra – it's one word but so powerful and without belief we have nothing. As I started my new job on Rescue Mediums I was asking my guides if I was up to the job as I was feeling a little nervous about working in front of cameras and being in a strange country away from my family; to say I was feeling out of my comfort zone is an understatement. However, Ruby thought otherwise and dictated this lovely poem to me:

Make a wish, as dreams can come true. All you have to do is Believe, with a capital B.

Watch your wings unfold as you soar through the universe, with your head held high. You are true to yourself and others.

Make a wish and reach for the stars. Your life is only beginning. You deserve the riches of the love and light that we, your angels, are sending.

All you need to do is Believe, with a capital B.

C is for Children Of The Light

"The soul is healed by being with children."

—ENGLISH PROVERB

Every child is special, but some are born to share their spiritual light with others and anyone who is a parent to one of these children cannot fail to notice how they are wise beyond their years and will often refer to their 'other Mummy', or have knowledge about a place they have never visited before in this lifetime. The world in which we live is going through an awakening of consciousness never experienced before. It is hard to comprehend but exciting at the same time and these children have been born to spread the word of why our world is changing and how important it is for us to move through this change with hope in our hearts. These children are part of a great evolution in the consciousness of humanity and I feel we will be reading more about special children's amazing abilities from a very early age. You will often read about them in the newspapers as they have stunned not only their parents, but also so-called experts. I believe that some of these children are the children of the new world.

A fabulous example that was in the paper recently was about a little boy of two-years old who can identify all 195 independent sovereign states on a map of the world and match them with their national flags. He can also read up to 500 words, going on to describe all major body organs and their functions, count to 200, identify shapes and explain volcanoes and shooting stars. If this isn't a 'star child' I will eat my hat! Read on to see what you think.

I have listed below the title that has been given to these children and a reference of what makes them different from other children. However, this list is not definitive, it is purely a guide and some children could be a combination of two or three types. For example, your child may be a Crystal child with some Rainbow qualities.

Indigo children

The 'oldest' of the gifted children, the term 'Indigo' was coined in the 1970s by Nancy Ann Tappe, a parapsychologist who devised a system to describe people's personalities according to the hue of their auras. She describes the Indigos as having differing traits such as informing their parents of who they are (as if they have been here before or are aware of why they are here right now). They are known as 'new wave' children who have strong spiritual and psychological attributes. They are not afraid of speaking out for what they believe in, speaking their truth at every opportunity. They often experience paranormal activity and some are known to be telepathic. Indigo children can appear antisocial to those who don't know them, and feel more comfortable with their own kind. They are sensitive souls and find dealing with authority a problem and therefore often struggle at school. Indigos can often suffer from learning difficulties and modern medical disorders such as ADHD.

Crystal children

These children were mainly brought to Earth around 1990 to 2010 and like the Indigo children they can be sensitive, telepathic and extremely perceptive. They are born into 'the golden ray of incarnation and evolution' so are gifted souls showing signs of being clairvoyant and natural healers from an early age. They are extremely forgiving, warm and caring and can reflect things back to the universe that are longer useful to them. Crystal children are advocates for love and peace on planet Earth and are representatives of who we once were.

Star children

Star children bring peace to Earth, are extremely intelligent and possess extrasensory abilities. It is said that star children have been sent from all areas of the universe to help the Earth and its inhabitants. Before their birth, star children have chosen parents who will support them and help develop their natural abilities. They have innate understandings of energy and are here on special assignment to assist in the rebirth of a higher dimensional Earth.

Rainbow children

Rainbow children are born with the full spectrum of rainbow colours in their auras. They are happy children who bring absolute joy and harmony to their parents and as they have never been incarnated before, they hold no karma. Rainbow children can see the good in everyone and are extremely intuitive. They can often read people's feelings and emotions and they have the gift of being able to manifest what they desire from the universe.

A true account of a very special child, Gemma

A good friend of mine has a beautiful daughter aged nine who I will call Gemma (as this is a favourite name of hers!) in order to protect her identity. She has vivid impressions of spirit who often appear to her 'out of the blue' and she normally takes this in her stride. However, my friend brought Gemma to meet me one day as she wanted some advice about a spirit who was appearing to Gemma in a scary and frightening manner. Gemma's Mum had kept a journal of her daughter's experiences and she has been good enough to let me have a copy so I can share her story with you.

23 March, 2012

Gemma was in her friend's garden playing. She came in and whispered to me that she had seen something. Later when we went home she said she had seen a man and thought he looked like a farmer. He wore a flat cap, a checked shirt and ripped jeans (not pre-ripped). He had a gun and was pointing it at the girls saying "Payback". Gemma heard loud bangs as he shot his gun at them but she realised that her friend couldn't see him, only she could, and somehow she knew that he couldn't hurt them even though she was very scared. When the girls were sitting upstairs in her friend's bedroom she heard a loud scraping on the wall, like a pitchfork being scraped down a board. I suggested that maybe someone was trying to get her attention but she said it wasn't a friendly feeling. She said that she hadn't shared any of what she had seen and felt with her friend, which I think was a good judgement from my wee woman.

A few days later Gemma saw the farmer again whilst at school. He was shooting at her and her friend. She was "creeped out" by it (her own words) but dealt with it well. She didn't tell her friend, but went to find a teacher she trusted and told her.

16th April, 2012

Gemma saw the farmer again at school and this time he strode towards her and scraped his pitchfork across her work and she heard the sound of ripping paper. (Afterwards, she said there was a rip at the corner of the sheet of paper she was working on but she is pretty sure it was there beforehand, although she couldn't say for definite.) She tells me that in her head she told him to leave her alone and he laughed. I do find this difficult, I am not happy that my little girl is experiencing such threatening scenes. She did see her wolf before the farmer appeared though, and I do think it's lovely that she associates the wolf with being protected now but it did leave her feeling upset.

When I went to pick her up from after school club she was very quiet and the club leader said she thought it was because her friend wasn't there that day. Gemma told the teacher she trusted about her experience and even though I feel it is a very private family thing, that we have kept quiet apart from in the confines of our immediate family, I think it's good that she can talk to this teacher at school if she is scared. I have to trust her judgement on this as she's very good at knowing what's right for her even though she is so young. (I still think this is a bit too young for my little girl to have to see this stuff.) I have sent healing to the school and imagined it surrounded in light. I have enlisted the help of Archangel Michael. I have suggested that when the wolf appears that she grounds herself and I feel she will manage this well.

18th April, 2012

Well the farmer has appeared again. This time it upset Gemma a lot. She was outside school and watched him as he shot a horse. It was particularly upsetting as he shot the horse in the stomach so the horse was in a great deal of pain and screaming like a horse would. He ran off across the field and through some hedges. The lovely thing was, though, that her wolf appeared before the farmer did and then arrived at the scene before her. The wolf then ran around the horse in circles before lying down across the horse where it had been shot.

21st April, 2012

We had arranged to meet Alison (Wynne-Ryder) today. I had contacted her after Gemma had seen a nasty vision and we were pretty unsettled about how things were developing. I wanted some advice from someone who might understand more about what my daughter was experiencing. I also thought it would help her to speak to someone else other than just me and her Dad. Gemma had seen Alison on the Rescue Mediums show on television so she was quite excited. We had a lovely few hours with Alison and she was great with Gemma. My daughter went through all the things she had seen and Alison gave us advice on how we can protect ourselves, especially Gemma, and what she should do if the farmer appeared again.

25th April, 2012

What a lovely and special thing that happened this evening. I had dropped my son off at rugby training. Gemma and I had been to Tesco shopping, and on the way back to get her brother, Gemma said that she hadn't seen anything since she had met with Alison. She was bothered about this as she was afraid that maybe somehow she had lost her gift. Even though it scared her sometimes she still wanted to be able to 'see'. We had a chat about this as I just wanted her to understand that ideally we'd rather she didn't see things that frightened her so much that she had to go and find an adult to talk to (e.g. her trusted teacher). I told her that she hadn't lost her gift and that in any event it was only a week since she had seen the last scene. Anyway, we parked up to wait for my son and Gemma was reading through a magazine we had bought in Tesco's. She looked up and went "Awww" and had a lovely big smile on her face. I was keen to see what she was looking at and leaned across. "You won't be able to see it," she said. She reminded me that Alison had said she felt Gemma would see the horse again in happier circumstances. Well, Gemma could see the horse jumping about and playing on the field and her wolf was with it! What a lovely thing to see. She was absolutely chuffed to bits. I asked her what colour the horse was and she said it was a bright white. (This was why it looked so bad in her original image as she could see the blood all over it where the farmer had shot it).

2nd May, 2012

This evening Gemma told me that she saw the farmer again today at school but it was very different. She was in class and she saw him standing outside in the garden area outside her classroom windows. She said that he looked tired and wet and looked like he had given up, as if he was thinking, "You win." Gemma said she remembered Alison saying that if she saw him again that she should send him lots of bright light so she did. She imagined a beautiful ball of light that moved from her to him, and got bigger as it went towards him. She wanted it to be blue after Archangel Michael so it was blue, rather than the usual white. She told him to "Walk into the light." She watched him go into it and said, "I don't think I'll be seeing him again." She was surprised that her wolf was not there this time, which was a first for her when she is seeing scenes like this. We talked about whether or not this was because she didn't need the protection so much on this one – who knows? But that's a fairly nice end to it, it seems.

Conclusion

I saw Gemma and her Mum a few days later and confirmed that Gemma didn't need to see her wolf all the time, but she should feel protected by him as he is her spirit guide animal and will always be there. I explained that you don't always need to see what you believe; for example, think of angels and God. We know they exist but we don't have to physically see them.

I find it incredible that such a young girl has had to endure such vivid and in some cases extremely frightening images with her third eye. Her Mum is wonderful, down-to-earth and a very spiritual soul herself. She was so worried about what her daughter was experiencing which is why she contacted me to see if I could help. I listened with horror as this little girl relayed what she had seen and felt, and I could see in her eyes how scared she was; but at the same time there was a maturity about her which gave her such strength and understanding about her gift. I knew that she was an old soul and possibly a crystal child with some rainbow abilities thrown in. When we discussed what had been happening, particularly with the farmer, I told Gemma that for some reason a part of his life was being played out in segments similar to a jigsaw puzzle and he wanted her to find the final piece to make the picture whole. She understood that the wolf was her spirit animal guide and I went through grounding and psychic protection with her; we did this together so I knew she understood what to do. I told her when she was frightened to hold an image of something lovely in her mind's eye, and as I was telling her this I could see beautiful brightly coloured butterflies around her. When I conveyed this to both Gemma and her mother they confirmed that the butterflies were something very special to Gemma, so I knew that she would find it easy to concentrate on an image of the butterflies.

I told her that the horse was now in spirit and she would see him looking well. The fact that her wolf animal guide was with the horse indicated that he helped the horse to go to the light and be happy and free of pain in the spirit world. As for the farmer, I knew from what Gemma was telling me was that he was attracted to her psychic light and was asking for help. For some reason he hadn't gone to the light when he should have done and what she saw was a snapshot of a part of his life that was unfolding before her very eyes. When she sent him the light and saw him no more, she knew she had finally found the last piece of the puzzle and the jigsaw was now complete. Once Gemma realised this and that he had no intention of hurting her, she was able to send him the light with the help of her spirit guide. She let me into a secret too, that Archangel Michael helped her. How comforting to know that the leader of the Archangels stepped in to protect such a special and brave little girl.

There are happier visions that Gemma wanted to share with me and I have her and her Mum's permission to let you into her world. Here were some questions that I posed to both of them, as I felt it would be good to understand how Gemma knew she had the gift and how she deals with it.

How do you feel about your gift and what would you say to other children who also have the gift?

I do see what I can do as a gift and I would say to other children, "Don't be afraid as it is a natural gift." I used to be frightened about what I saw but I know they can't hurt me.

What is the most frightening thing you have seen?

The farmer was the most frightening one but also two people I saw where the man shot the woman but they couldn't see me.

What has been the most special thing about your gift?

Seeing my friend's late granddad. I saw him carrying some shopping bags and with a big smile on his face. I had never seen him before but somehow I knew it was her granddad. I described him to her and she said it did sound like him. When I told her I could see him with shopping bags, she said that he had died suddenly while out shopping.

What has surprised you the most about your gift?

I see 'the little people' and they are very cute.

Wow! How do you feel, seeing the little people and where do you usually see them?

When I first saw them I was surprised but not frightened. I usually see them in a tree in the woods.

Do you feel different to everyone else?

I don't feel different to my friends and even though my family tell me I'm special I don't feel I am. I didn't tell anyone for a long time as I felt that other people wouldn't believe me.

Do any of your friends know you have the gift?

There is only one girl in the school and one of the teachers who know what I can do. Some of my friends say I am odd when I talk about some things, but I usually keep spiritual things separate as I don't know whether they would understand.

What advice would you give to children who feel they have the gift?

Please don't keep it from your Mum and Dad and don't be afraid to tell them as it was okay when I told my Mum. She was great and my Dad doesn't normally believe in spiritual things but he believed me as I am his daughter.

Was it a relief to tell your parents what you can do?

Oooh, yes....

What do you feel about ouija boards?

I don't like them at all as I don't like the thought of dead people coming into my house and not going away. I mean, you could have King Henry the VIII coming into the house and then there could be a door open and a big queue of them coming in.

Questions and answers with Gemma's Mum

How did you feel when Gemma first told you about her gift?

Honestly? I felt so guilty for not having spoken to her about spirituality before. I grew up experiencing all kinds of things when I was a child and was lucky enough to have a Mum who also had the gift. I wish I had told Gemma about my own experiences when I was young. I suppose I was trying to protect my little girl from something I felt may frighten her. Little did I know! When I asked her why she hadn't told me earlier about what she could do, she said she felt that people wouldn't believe her as she said it felt different.

Gemma has shared some of her more frightening visions with me. How would you describe what she saw?

I liken it to a vibration of something that had happened in the past, similar to a scene being replayed on television and something that I would never allow Gemma to watch.

What was significant about the time when Gemma felt she could share her experiences with you?

It was when you attuned me to Reiki and I shared what I had felt like on my special healing day with Gemma. Apparently that was the turning point as Gemma said she thought that Reiki sounded a very special word and at that point she felt she could speak to me.

What was it that struck you the most about what Gemma had to say?

The fact that how did she know to keep all this to herself, inside of her, and not to say anything to anyone? When I asked her about this she said she kept it to herself because she felt it wasn't an everyday thing and she hadn't heard any of her friends talk about spirits, orbs, etcetera so she realised it was different.

How do you feel now about Gemma's gift?

Relieved that she has told me what she has experienced so I can help in any way I can and she knows she has mine and her Dad's support 100%. As a child, sensing spirit was normal to me as I grew up in a household where some of our family also had the gift and we could talk about anything to do with spirituality.

Oh, you were so lucky! I didn't have anyone I could go to as a child so it must be a relief that Gemma can talk to you about spirituality and that you understand what she is going through.

Oh it is, and although some of the things she has experienced have frightened her, there are more things that are absolutely beautiful like when she sees the 'little people', her wolf and auras.

Earlier extracts from Gemma's Mum's journal

30ᵗʰ July, 2011

Having deleted the Aura Photo App from my daughter's iPod it turned out that she really liked it so I promised I'd put it on again. I pointed out gently that it didn't really take a photograph of your aura and she said she realised that but what she really liked was the area on the app that listed the meaning of the colours. She told me she could see real auras so she knew already! She said she could see most of the colours and, when she can't, she has a good look over the person, closes her eyes and then sees the colours. She knows that auras change colour and told me that mine was a greeny-blue.

I asked if she could see orbs as I had just downloaded a book on orbs onto the Kindle so it was timely. She said she could and saw them often mostly outdoors in wooded areas. She says she can see her own when she closes her eyes (must ask more about this!). I showed her some photos from the book and she said they looked exactly like the ones she sees. I explained that they can be angels, your guardian angel or your spirit guide, etcetera. She says she sees a lot of them around her friends when they are upset or hurt. When her friend flipped over and fell from a tree at school, Gemma could see a lot of orbs around her. She says she sees our family's auras when we are all together – she sees pink outlines (must ask more about this too!).

She said she had meant to tell me but kept forgetting. Gemma told me she knows that Reiki is a spiritual thing from what I had told her, so that's why she told me about her gift. She hasn't told any of her friends yet. When she told her brother that his aura showed that he was a bit spiritual he questioned this as he doesn't think he is, although he is quite open minded. She said, "Well, your body is saying something different!"

31ˢᵗ July, 2011

Gemma told me that she sees 'little people' sometimes. Little people who fly, have little wings. Fairies fell off my radar years ago so this was quite new for me – although Diana Cooper's book dealt with it so that was helpful and of course if Gemma tells me she can see them, then that's all I need to believe. A lot to think about!

I asked Gemma if she saw big people. She said she did, but not very often and when she does they are normally with family. They look like people but 'different colours'. They know she can see them (I asked). She said that she had seen Mum (passed) with me, and another lady she didn't know with Mum, when she was in the hospice. She had also seen her friend's granddad with her – at least, she thinks that's who it might have been. She also saw another friend's cat around her. About the other lady with Mum - she told me about her when we got back from holiday. She said that she didn't know the lady but then asked me what my auntie had looked like. I told her she was very little with short curly hair. She said that the lady she had seen was very small, wore a dress and had tiny shoes. The next day I showed her a photograph of my auntie with some other family members and she pointed to the lady she had seen with Mum at the hospice. When I asked her what colour my auntie's dress had been, she said that when she doesn't see them in colour, she calls them 'ghosts'. I have asked her what the little people look like. What she described sounded like how I would have envisioned a fairy – little people who fly. She also said they wear unusual clothes and hats, and that they appear either inside or outside the trees.

August/September/October, 2011

I think I am trying to find a balance between asking Gemma what she is seeing and not bothering her. I find her abilities delightful and exciting but I do still want to take care of her and make sure she is okay. She is opening my mind, too! Gemma says she sees 'shadow people', sometimes in broad daylight. She also said she had seen a couple of little people in a tree in the wild area – the boy one was lounging, chilling out and staring at her.

15th March, 2012

It's been a good long while since I wrote some notes. Things have just been moving along. Gemma still sees orbs and auras (although we don't talk about it much). I suppose I'm just trying to seek a balance on what I should ask her, and how often. I did ask her about 'shadow people' though after I had seen one myself and was quite blown away by it (it was a thrill for me, but nothing since, mostly an awareness and lots of stuff out of the corner of my eye) – but

Gemma sees a lot of them. It seems there is a lot of activity of this type around the school and also in her tutor's garden which is near to the school field. Mostly the shadow people ignore her but she told me this week that there has been a time when one of them ran up to her with its arms up and seemed to run through her. She didn't like that much at all. She doesn't like her tutor's garden in the dark – I asked her how many she had seen in the tutor's garden and she said there could be as many as six or seven at any one time. This week we learned that things have moved on again. Gemma has been seeing a scene – an 'event' – maybe a 'ghost memory'. She sees a man standing over a woman who is crouched down on the floor, saying, "No, no, no." Initially she told me that he had something in his hand but didn't know what, but by the third time she saw them she could see it was a gun. Not really what Mummy wants to hear. The man was wearing black leather trousers, a long-sleeved black top with a turtle neck. At this point we are talking a lot about psychic protection and she understands this as we have talked about it before. She also told a trusted teacher that she thought it would help to have a caring adult at school for when she gets afraid, and she has been great!

16th March, 2012

Gemma tells me that she saw that awful scene again today. This time the man shot the woman. She told me that the woman said, "Take me." We chatted about this and the possibility that she was protecting someone or something, perhaps a child. Gemma was scared rigid, needless to say, and she told her trusted teacher who, like me, thought that perhaps this would be the end of it. I hope this is the case but then again if it is a ghost memory why would it disappear? Why would my little girl be shown this? I asked Gemma if she had watched anything on the television that would have put these images into her head but she said not and I believe her, as it's not the kind of thing we would let her watch. The scene, combined with others she has seen, is making me think she's in a different place and seeing stuff we would rather she didn't. I don't get this at all. Why doesn't her guide protect her from this and, if not, why can't this be the case? The main thing is that even though she is scared at the time, she is being quite strong about it. I gave her Reiki healing this evening and it was beautiful.

21st March, 2012

Things seem to have settled and long may that last. She loves her gift and doesn't want to switch off, but the scenes she has been seeing are a little extreme for me. Gemma tells me that the biggest orb she has ever seen was at her Nana's funeral in the church, by her coffin. It was rainbow colours about a foot and a half. It wasn't round though, it was more like a hexagon. It was "Really gorgeous."

6th April, 2012

Gemma and I went walking with our dog in Anderton. On the way back to the car park, she told me she had heard voices and I could tell she was a little uneasy. There were people close by that I could just about hear but she said it wasn't them, as it was like three voices around us in a triangle but she couldn't see anyone. I asked if she had any names and she said the name Darren. She wasn't comfortable so we wanted to move on. I asked that whoever was with us would stay where they were and let us go ahead without them and I felt that they did. Gemma then looked across at some trees and asked why there was a man standing behind the trees. The trees were actually lots of little saplings that were easy to see through. I said I couldn't see anyone so it must be someone that only she could see. She wondered if it was Darren. We moved on and she said that the man started to come towards us. We sat down on our 'wood mouse' bench (where we had seen a lot of little tiny wood mice a couple of weeks ago) and had a chat about it. My daughter said she felt that this is something she just needs to get used to, as she doesn't want to lose the ability to 'see'. She felt it was a lot easier dealing with it when I am there with her. I suggested that she lets 'them' know that she is too young to speak to them, by saying it out loud in her head firmly.

15th April, 2012

My sister and I were chatting about power animals earlier. On the way back from dropping her off at the airport Gemma told me something new. She kept seeing what she thought was a husky dog in her mind. It turned out it wasn't a husky after all, as I searched Google images and found some wolf photos and asked her if that was what she saw and she confirmed that yes, it was. She had never seen a picture of a wolf before.

I checked on Amazon for a book I had seen on animal spirit guides and in the wolf section one of the things it said was that "If a wolf shows up it means 'You are being spiritually and psychically protected at all times'." Gemma gave me a big smile when she heard this.

So there you have it, a very enlightening time for a lovely down-to-earth family who have a little girl with a tremendous gift. Now that Gemma understands how to protect herself in order to avoid any 'nasties' coming forward again, she can enjoy her gift and now sees it as such. I know that when she grows up she will become a very talented medium who will help a lot of people. I feel blessed that her Mum trusted me so I could tell her story in order to help other parents of psychic children.

This next account from a 'child of the light' is from Lauren Dower who is a beautiful and intelligent young woman with her head screwed on. What happened to her is the most incredible story of how our spirit guides can give us succinct signs of their presence. The messages that Lauren has received are like no other I have heard or witnessed. I have my own feelings on this, which I write about at the end of Lauren's story. I decided to write her experience in her own words so I asked her to dictate what happened. Read on to find out what you make of this.

Lauren

"As far back as I can remember, for some reason I have never liked the story or the film of Alice in Wonderland. I saw the film when I was little but it frightened me so much I never saw it again and I have done everything in my power to avoid reading the book. I never knew quite why the story made me shudder but there is one scene I was petrified of, and that is when Alice falls down the rabbit hole. When I saw this when I was little, it felt like it was me falling down that rabbit hole, going down and down and down and the fear has never left me. I know it sounds strange and no matter how many times I have tried to be rational about it and thought deeply into why I had this fear, it still made no sense particularly as I have always loved stories so much.

"I suppose the only way you could put it in layman's terms is that I was just not inclined towards it. I remember when I was about eight years old, I used to go to a place called the Crocky Trail which was on the way to Chester. We used to pass a hotel on the journey which had a sign outside with the picture of a big fat grinning Cheshire Cat on it. Seeing that sign and the feelings I had around it as a child have stuck with me forever.

"Things lately though have been extremely bizarre. No matter what I do, I seem to be linked or connected in some way to the story of Alice in Wonderland or to Lewis Carroll himself. Certain things just seemed natural and I never gave them a second thought such as moving house with Mum and Dad to Daresbury (near to Runcorn and Warrington) which is Lewis Carroll's birthplace. The first incident was when I started a job as a waitress at a pub in Daresbury. I was in the room on my own cleaning tables when I felt an eerie sense around me like there was someone standing nearby. As I looked up, I was drawn to some pictures on the wall depicting the story of Alice in Wonderland. There were four of them, and each showed a particular scene of the story. I didn't think about this too much but I did tell my parents when I got home.

"The thing is, I am not a superstitious person and I always look for a reason behind everything, but I was really freaked out when the next thing happened. I was reading Literature at university for my degree, and not long after the pub incident, my reading list from university came through. To my amazement, mine included Alice in Wonderland. I remember feeling quite disturbed by this, as I didn't want to read the book. My Dad was joking around saying, 'You are doing Literature so you have a strong link with Lewis Carroll and, let's face it, he has written one of the best-loved books in literature'. However, I did everything in my power to avoid reading it and I managed this by getting a First in my degree.

"I remember arguing with Dad as I said there is no point to the story as it just seemed to be nonsense. He said it was about good and evil. Even when I had to sit listening to lectures about the story at university I had the weirdest feeling that I was being 'forced' to read it by Lewis Carroll's spirit. On the other side of the coin, though, was when others were looking into his life history and calling him a paedophile I felt quite protective about this and felt he should be left alone. I just couldn't explain my feelings on any of it and it did freak me out a little if I'm being honest.

"The next thing that happened was when I had been to the careers office at university and they were asking me loads of questions about what I wanted to do and I didn't really know. I remember feeling out of my depth and I had that awful feeling again of falling down the rabbit hole. I have always been driven and been in control of my life but the thought of not knowing what I wanted to do in life frightened me.

"Not long after, I was working at the pub when I was doing my waitressing job cleaning tables and I was in a different area of the restaurant to where I am normally. There was a shelf in the room that contained numerous pictures which were coloured black, white and red - similar to the colours on a pack of cards. I noticed that one of the pictures said 'Off with her head', and I realised then that the pictures were taken from Alice in Wonderland. For some reason one of the pictures stood out to me even though it was the same size as the others and in the same frame. Maybe it was because this one included a quote and I love quotes; I have positive quotes all over my bedroom. As I looked closer, I could see that in the left-hand corner was a picture of Alice and there was also a picture of the Cheshire Cat in the tree. The quote was:

Alice came to a fork in the road. "Which road do I take?" she asked.
"Where do you want to go?" responded the Cheshire Cat. "I don't know",
Alice answered. "Then," said the cat, "it doesn't matter."

I felt comforted, which surprised me. It was a warm sensation inside of me and I thought what a fabulous quote for me at this time, so I knew instantly that instead of getting upset and stalling I had to go with it and keep progressing and that everything will turn out in the right way. I loved the quote so much that I tried to take a picture of it, but as soon as I had the camera up on my `phone to take the picture, the `phone died on me. I didn't think too much about it at the time but what I did think was, well, maybe Alice in Wonderland isn't a novel of total rubbish after all as I felt this was a definite and positive message for me at that time in my life.

"About two days later when I was back in work I was carrying plates past the shelf again, and as I glanced over I noticed to my horror that the picture with the quote had disappeared. My first instinct was to go the manager to tell him someone had stolen the picture but I realised that it would be too big a picture to carry out of the restaurant without anyone noticing it; and apart from that, the other photos were there so why would someone just want to take that particular one? I decided to ask the other waitresses what had happened to the picture with the quote and had anyone moved it, but none of them knew what I was talking about. There was no clear indication of where the picture had been on the shelf. There was no area of dust in the shape of the picture and there was no gap as to where it stood. To be honest, the whole thing seemed so strange that I felt queasy inside and I started to question myself as to whether I had actually seen the picture although, in my heart, I knew I had. What was going on? Also, how would I know the quote when I have never read the book before or heard anything about it in my lectures because at that time I hadn't studied Lewis Carroll because Alice in Wonderland was the last novel on the curriculum so it must have been around January; that was the time when we had to decide on a path for the next six months of term. I was determined now to find out what on Earth was going on and if that quote did actually exist so when I got home I 'Googled' it and there it was – a definite quote from the story of Alice in Wonderland.

"Not long after, I was on a work placement through university at the Cheshire Wildlife Trust. During the second week of the placement I was sifting through membership forms and amongst them was a card like a greeting card and on the front was the Cheshire Cat in the tree! This time I grabbed hold of it instinctively as I thought 'This one isn't getting away' and I asked my colleague who was sitting opposite me why a greeting card would be in the middle of the forms. She just shook her head and said, 'I don't know,' and carried on with her work. I had never mentioned anything that had happened to me previously with anyone at the placement. When I opened the card all it said was 'From Peter'. Nothing else! I thought how very strange – no message, just that.

"I also find it uncanny that I also worked at The Daresbury Hotel which is where I met my boyfriend. The first time I met him he was dressed up as The White Rabbit! He has to wear the costume to greet visitors to the hotel. I always said to him that I felt an angel had sent him to me.

"The latest occurrence happened recently when I was out shopping with Mum and Dad, and we were sitting in Costa's having a coffee. My Dad had just purchased a new mobile 'phone and I said 'Can I have a look at it?', as I wanted one of these myself – you can read books on them, so I clicked on the books app. To my surprise it said '78% downloading'. I thought this was funny because I hadn't thought I'd downloaded anything but when I looked, there it was – Chapter One of Alice in Wonderland."

My feelings about the story

Events for Lauren were certainly getting curiouser and curiouser. I asked her how she felt in general as a child and she said that she had always felt different somehow and she believed that there was something else 'out there' but didn't know quite what. She also feels that she is here to help others and I don't doubt this at all. She told me that the character Alice from the book was based on the daughter of the author's friends, and her name was Alice Liddell. When she showed me a picture of Alice and a picture of herself at around the same age (about 9), the similarity between the two is uncanny. At first I thought that Alice could possibly be a previous life of Lauren's, but after she had told me her story and I had typed it up, I did an hour clairvoyant reading for her.

There were many messages for Lauren from the reading but there were also images I was being shown which I felt linked into Lewis Carroll. However, as these were quite disjointed I decided to do some research of my own on the author to see what I could dig up. I felt that the messages that were coming through were clues as to what I would find, and we both decided to do our own initial research and then look at what we have both investigated. This is going to take a lot of time, effort and patience but I feel that we will reap rewards as I was being given this information from spirit for a reason.

During the reading, the feeling I was getting was that he cared about Lauren and was showing her signs to help guide her along her path. Rather than being someone to be frightened of, he is her spirit guide and is very protective around her. At the end of the reading I asked my pendulum this very question and we received our confirmation that 'Yes, indeed, Lewis Carroll is Lauren's spirit guide'. I do feel though that she also has strong links with Alice Liddell and I will do everything I can to find out what it is. I know that we are already in possession of a few jigsaw pieces but we need the rest to be able to tell the full story. I know it doesn't stop here and there is plenty more to come in this delicious true story – maybe in another book! One of the things prominent in Lauren's reading was something about a wasp, and I had a feeling as if I was on a train. When I mentioned this to Lauren she said she hadn't seen any or been stung by one, but spirit kept repeating it; the train didn't mean anything either so after she had gone I did some investigating and found something very interesting. Apparently when Lewis Carroll had written Through the Looking Glass, he had included a chapter entitled The Wasp in a Wig. However John Tenniel, who did the illustrations for Carroll's Alice's Adventures in Wonderland and Through the Looking Glass objected to it, so Carroll took out the whole chapter, and The Wasp in a Wig was known thereafter as 'the lost chapter'. Interestingly, on the 1st June, 1870, Tenniel wrote to Carroll as follows:

My dear Dodgson (Carroll's real name),

I think that when the jump occurs in the railway scene you might very well make Alice lay hold of the goat's beard as being the object nearest to her hand – instead of the old lady's hair. The jerk would actually throw them together. Don't think me brutal, but I am bound to say that 'the wasp' chapter does not interest me in the least, and I can't see my way to a picture. If you want to start on the book, I can't help thinking with all the submissions that this is your opportunity.

In an agony of haste,
Yours sincerely, J. Tenniel

I am sporting a Cheshire Cat grin as I type this! An adventure is unfolding for Lauren and I feel that Lewis Carroll is behind it in a good way; she is learning to trust, go with the flow and to live in the moment. One thing I feel in my heart is that he wants people to know 'the real Lewis Carroll' – there have been so many different accounts written about his life, some good and some not so good, but how much of the man himself is really known? Maybe he wants to tell his own story – who knows? For now, I am honoured that Lauren has trusted me with her story and I feel excited regarding any developments in the future. I know that some of the other clues given to me by the spirit world when I did Lauren's reading will uncover some very interesting developments and I feel extremely excited about it all.

Lauren will have lots of fun finding out what her mission in life is with the guidance and protection of her very special spirit guide.

C is also for Clairvoyance

"The most pathetic person in the world is someone who has sight but has no vision."

—HELEN KELLER

Clairvoyance means 'clear vision' and developing any form of psychic ability is a personal journey for each and every one of us. For me, meditation will always be the key to understanding my inner self. Through experience, I have learned to still my mind and to 'simply be'. It was through a vivid dream and subsequent meditations that I met my main spirit guides Zamil and Ruby, and I feel that since developing my psychic abilities in general, I have gained a better understanding of my life's purpose.

Being clairvoyant means that as well as using my mediumistic skills to communicate with spirit, I have a clear vision of future events which are sometimes called premonitions. These are given to me either in full colour image form similar to that of camera 'snaps' or I will be given words, names or dates, etcetera. In effect I am seeing with my 'third eye', which is the chakra in the middle of the forehead. Before doing a clairvoyant reading I 'open up' to the spirit world using the method of opening up the chakras which are energy points in my body. Prior to opening up the chakras, I ensure that I am grounded and that I put psychic protection around myself and meditate with my spirit guides who give me information known as a 'premonitions list' prior to me meeting the client. Once the client has arrived, I put them at their ease, explain what to expect from their reading, and tell them which divination tool I will use in conjunction with my mediumistic skills.

I enjoy psychometry which is where I hold a personal item belonging to my client such as a piece of jewellery, mobile 'phone, keys and so on, as the object retains that person's energy or emotions and I can do a reading from that. In conjunction with psychometry, I carry out Tarot and angel card readings. I don't see what I do as a technique - it is a natural gift bestowed on me from the spirit world. I believe in the information they give me 100% and feel blessed that I am able to pass on their loving guidance to others.

C is for Crystals

"Crystals grew inside rock like arithmetic flowers. They lengthened and spread, added plane to plane in an awed and perfect obedience to an absolute geometry that even stones, maybe only the stones, understood."

—ANNIE DILLARD

I use crystals on a daily basis when taking classes, meditating and to promote a positive theme within my home and work environment. Read on to learn more about how crystals can help us in our daily life.

The first thing to do is to choose your crystal. Once you have decided which type of crystal to buy, such as one that will assist in bringing love into your life like rose quartz, close your eyes and ask the angels to help to guide you towards the crystal that is meant for you. When you open your eyes, see which crystal seems the most prominent. If you are torn between two or three crystals, it's a good idea to hold each one in turn, feeling and sensing their energy and healing vibration. The one that 'calls out to you' in terms of warmth, healing energies, or a tingling in your hand, is yours!

Before working with your crystal, it will need to be cleansed and charged. In order to do this, wash it in lightly salted water and place it outside during the day (but not when the sun is extremely hot as you will not want to either start a fire or fade certain crystals such as amethyst or citrine). I leave my crystal out overnight so it can be charged by the magic of the moonlight. Ensure the crystal is only handled by you. If someone else picks it up or handles it in any way you will have to go through the ritual of cleansing it all over again. If you prefer, after cleansing your crystal you can use the same format by placing your crystal on a window sill.

There are certain crystals that you will not be able to cleanse by washing them, such as selenite which is water soluble, and layered crystals such as the beautiful angel wing calcite. Using your intuition is vital regarding crystal care, so if you feel parts of the crystal would break away if you cleansed it in water, then refrain from doing so. Certain crystals such as citrine and kyanite are self-cleansing, so you will never need to cleanse them yourself.

Crystals are full of magic and mystery and have beautiful but powerful qualities. They never lose colour, beauty or value and in many ancient civilisations this aligned them with the spirit world and Heaven. I find it amazing that the first written accounts of crystal healing came from the ancient Egyptians who gave detailed information about using gemstones such as malachite for healing. When choosing an 'angel crystal' ask the angels to help to guide you to the one that is meant for you. This could be a simple act such as being drawn to a particular crystal, or one that seems to glow or radiate in some way. Once you have purchased your crystal, you can ask the angels of light, love and protection to place their energy within the crystal.

Here is a brief description of some of the 'angelic' crystals available. I have chosen these not just for their qualities, but because they are usually readily available and not too expensive.

Angel aura quartz

This crystal is lovely and the angelic meaning for this crystal is 'Your guardian angel'. It's a great stone to use in therapy sessions or any form of healing. Angel aura quartz can help you become aware of nature spirits and fairies as well as awakening your spiritual awareness. Emotionally, this lovely stone releases inhibition, releases stress of any kind and brings peace to emotional issues and discord. Angel aura quartz is opalescent in colour.

Angelite

If you hold angelite in your hand whilst meditating it can increase a conscious connection to the angelic realms. This beautiful pale blue stone promotes tranquillity, inner peace and calm. It can enhance telepathic skills which can assist you in interacting with others at a much higher emotional level. It also helps you to release anything that no longer serves your higher good.

Celestite

This is usually blue or white in colour. It can help you to focus on the highest realms of Heavenly light. It promotes a sunny, joyful disposition and brings with it peace and tranquillity, and is a master teacher for the new age. Celestite links strongly with the celestial guardians, and I love to hold a piece of celestite when communicating with the celestial realms.

Prehnite

This is one of my favourite stones and one which I use regularly especially when I am treating a client with angelic healing as well as in meditation. Prehnite attunes to divine energies and can show you the way forward on your own spiritual path. It calms, boosts the immune system and it can alleviate nightmares, phobias and deep-rooted fears. It is a beneficial stone for hyperactive children. Prehnite is usually a soft apple-green colour although it can also be a darker green, yellow and white.

Quartz – Golden Rutilated (Angel Hair)

This is a beautiful stone, golden in colour with tiny veins running through it which is why it is often known as 'Angel Hair'. I always have a piece of this in my meditation room, when healing and during my Angel Work-shops. 'Angel Hair' heightens the energy of other quartz stones and is an important healing stone. It illuminates the soul, removes barriers to spiritual growth and soothes dark moods, offering relief from fears, phobias and anxiety. Golden Rutilated Quartz also aids respiratory difficulties and is a balancing stone for a sad or weak heart.

Clear quartz

A magical stone, its fabulous healing energies are often overlooked. Clear quartz raises energy to the highest possible level, enhancing psychic abilities, bringing them to the fore. It is a powerful healing stone, aids concentration and is a deep soul cleanser. It is also good for placing on top of angel or Tarot cards as a means of cleansing the deck.

Ruby

Well of course I had to add ruby, as this is the name of one of my guides! Ruby is readily available. Its colour is transparent red. The angel for ruby is Archangel Uriel. Ruby was said to be the most precious of all the gemstones that God created. It is 'Lord of Gems' and was used in the breastplate of the high priest. Ruby instils in the wearer a passion for life, courage, perseverance and positive leadership qualities. It is a stone for pioneers and the brave-hearted and stands for raw power and passion for life. Psychologically, ruby brings spiritual devotion through selfless service to others. It releases the soul's true potential.

Seraphinite

Seraphinite is a beautiful crystal whose name means 'the seraphim' as it contains white streaks which often appear as angelic silvery feathers, angel wings or angelic beings. Seraphinite is a very powerful healing stone. It activates angelic contact to the highest realms of healing, assisting you to succeed without struggling by harmonising the desires of the heart into alignment with your soul's true desires. It helps to dispel negative emotions and is especially useful during relationship problems.

D is for Dreaming

"There is a divination concerning some things in dreams not incredible."

—ARISTOTLE

Sleep is essential to our wellbeing as the body repairs itself and there is nothing as revitalising as a good night's sleep. If I have a sleepless night or haven't slept properly for a while I can get irritable and feel unwell. Think about what you are eating or drinking before going to bed. Absolute no-nos are stimulants such as coffee or alcohol. Also avoid heavy meals, fatty foods, cheese or chocolate – unless you want to be awake for most of the night as your digestion system will be working overtime. So what happens when we are asleep?

I find dreams absolutely fascinating and have always had vivid dreams as far back as I can remember. It always intrigued me how some dreams stay with me for days afterwards whereas others seemed to come and go and no matter how much I tried to remember them, the information had gone the minute I got out of bed. I believe that we are only meant to remember certain dreams as they have symbolic meanings and could be answers or clues to what is going on in our lives at this very time.

In order to remember details of your dreams, always have a pen and paper by your bedside so you can jot down salient notes. I write mine down as soon as I can, and then I write them up properly in my own dream journal. I also have a dream book, or dream dictionary as they are some-times called. If I feel I have had a dream that has an inner meaning that I cannot decipher myself, I will look it up in my dream book and it usually denotes something that is going on in my life at that time.

Sleep paralysis has happened to me lots of times over the years and I remember as a child lying in bed fully awake but not being able to move. I was so frightened, but I couldn't speak or shout out. If anyone has experi-enced this, you will know it can be a very frightening experience. So what is sleep paralysis? It is the inability to move at all, although you are fully conscious. From a health point of view it is nothing to worry about as it is purely your body which is not moving smoothly through the stages of sleep. Sleep paralysis usually lasts no longer than a couple of minutes although it can seem much longer.

When I dream, I sense what I call 'normal dreams'. These are usually dreams with symbolic meanings attributed to my past or the present. I also have dreams which are so vivid I feel I am actually there, and I have had visions in these dreams of places I will visit in the future; when I go there I will often get a sense of déjà vu that accompanies it.

Astral travel is an interpretation of an out-of-body experience where a person can exist in an astral body which is separate from the physical body, which means they are capable of travelling outside it. Some people believe this is attributed to the afterlife where the person's consciousness or soul's journey is described as an out-of-body experience. No-one knows whether near-death experiences are a glimpse into the afterlife, a place of tranquillity between our world and the next, a sneak preview into a different realm, or a hallucination. However, one thing that is a common theme amongst all those who have had a near-death experience is that they felt transformed and it had a profound effect on them. Some of the things people say are that they experienced meeting a loved one who was in spirit. Others see themselves in a different world where there is no pain or worry and some people give accounts of feeling as if they were weightless and 'floating' around.

When we astral travel in our dreams, we can find ourselves in different places around the globe that we have never visited before, yet we can describe them in detail. People will give accounts of flying around and then choosing somewhere to land. When they wake up they often give a blow by blow account of where they have been. Some people often see their own body from either outside it or above it, looking down on it.

Prophetic dreams are those that seem to tell the future. I have had several prophetic dreams in the past particularly when working on the Rescue Mediums show. The following example proved to contain clues about what we found during our walkabout and how we brought the investigation to a fruitful close.

I was in a kitchen that I didn't recognise and knew there was something wrong. I could hear a flapping noise and as I looked over towards the kitchen window I could see a white dove in distress as it tried to make its escape out of the window. I ran over to it, trying to do everything in my power to release it but to no avail. I realised that the poor thing was injured and I woke up feeling really upset that I couldn't help it.

The dream was extremely vivid and in full colour – I truly felt as if I were there and I mentioned this when reading out my premonitions to the homeowner. When Jackie and I started our walkabout in the house and I saw the kitchen I had shivers down my spine as it was exactly as I had seen in my dream. There were also bird ornaments hanging from the ceiling which was uncanny. During our walkabout we saw a large feather on the wall pointing down towards the basement; we both shouted out excitedly as I had drawn a feather exactly like it on one of my psychic drawings which I had called 'strength'. Was this a message for us from our spirit guides telling us that we needed all our strength for this investigation? The entity in the property certainly felt very strong because we had experienced strong physical pain and I could smell something disgusting – it was obvious that the spirit was trying to tell us something; I also felt as if I were in the ground down below and kept feeling angry, like I was fighting with someone, and at one point I felt as if I'd had all the wind knocked out of me.

We knew we needed to be in the basement in order to carry out the rescue due to the clue of the eagle feather pointing downwards, but we felt so off-balance that we had to both sit on the floor. The trapped spirit was an angry male, and when he overshadowed Jackie she shouted, "I'm going to die." I knew it was him speaking through her and in the episode the viewer can hear me saying, "You are already dead, I can see you in a uniform – I am going to guide you along the path to the light – you need to go to the light." It took immense strength to get him over, and once we compared the story with independent research it was extremely poignant. He was a Scottish man who had emigrated to Canada with his family in the early 1900s, and they moved into the house in which our homeowners now live. Both he and his son enlisted and fought in WW1 on the Western Front and had to endure appalling conditions in the deep trenches, such as rats and the awful stink of rotting human excrement. The son was shot by a German sniper at the age of eighteen and as his father was suffering from a debilitating disease he was taken to hospital by boat, having to leave his son in the shell-torn fields of Flanders. But what was the message behind my vivid dream of the dove? At the Show and Tell we explained that the injured bird I had seen in my dream denoted a trapped spirit and the soul's release in death, together with the release of twenty-one doves as a tribute to the fallen heroes of the war, uniting the two meanings. Neither Jackie nor I could stop our tears falling as we watched the show for the first time. The viewer can see the soldier walking to the light with a white dove flying behind him as a mark of respect. The editors as usual, had done an absolutely sterling job in putting the show together.

Here are a few accounts shared by friends...

Lucy

"I have very vivid dreams. One I've been having lately keeps on showing me blogs, diaries, books and basically anything to do with writing. I don't know if that's a hint or anything.

"I've also had other very vivid dreams where loved ones who have passed visit me while sleeping. The dreams are very real. I can feel them when they hug me and have clear conversations sometimes. When my beloved cat Prowler died last year I had a dream where my late father-in-law came to me in a dream holding Prowler and smiling. It comforted me greatly."

Simon

"I had a dream a while ago in which I sold my house to live in a block of apartments on the top floor; yesterday I was speaking to a customer who is working from their apartment at Salford Quays and they are going to rent it out so are staying there for a few days to get it ready. I 'Google Street Mapped' their apartment so I could see where they were, and it is exactly the same building I had in my dream, although they are on the first floor and not the top, but exact opposite ends. I instantly recognised the building the moment I saw it. Very strange!"

Recurring dreams are repetitive in nature with little variation in the story or theme. They can be either positive or negative, and if the latter they could indicate something that remains negative or unresolved in waking life. I have had a recurring dream for years about living near water – I can see the lovely view from the window of a house I am in. Just lately, the dream has switched to me being in a strange house that I have never been in before, but I know it is mine. Most of the house is nice and light, but there is one room that seems dark and needs a lot of redecorating. Maybe I am being told that there is something I need to deal with in waking life, and once this has been sorted then the whole house will be light and inviting.

Most of us have experienced a nightmare, waking up in a sweat or even shouting out. Nightmares could occur because of real life trauma and they can be extremely frightening. Remember, though, what you are dreaming about is not always what occurs in waking life. As in normal dreams, look up the content of your nightmare in a dream book to determine how you can deal with the problem. For example, dreaming of death doesn't necessarily mean someone dies. Very often, as in Tarot, death means 'out with the old and in with the new'.

Certain dreams seem quite common such as being chased, where you are trying to outwit your pursuer. If you look into the meaning of this dream it could indicate someone you are frightened of in waking life, or that you are trying to run away from pressure, fears or stresses. Dreaming of death can be extremely scary but it usually means that a situation in waking life has died a death and you need to sever ties with it, or it could mean that you feel anger towards the person who has 'died' in your dream and you may decide to sever relationships with that person. Flying is another common dream that can denote wanting release from things in your life that are holding you back. These could be money worries, not being happy in your work or lack of self-worth. However from a more positive point of view, dreaming of flying can also signify freedom and independence.

If you dream of a house, it could be a representation of yourself and what is going on in your life. For example, the kitchen is the source of nourishment, the bedroom is part of the mind you go to when feeling stressed, and the walls of the house denote your own mental protection against life. I have many dreams of being in a house that I seem to recognise but it is not my own home, some of the rooms are bright and decorated nicely and others are darker. This could indicate that I am procrastinating about something in my life and, once I have dealt with it, the dark rooms will eventually become lighter.

Dreaming of insects is extremely common and could be niggling things that you need to deal with in your waking life. Have you ever dreamed that you are naked? Don't worry, you are not alone! This could mean that in waking life you feel vulnerable around a certain situation or person or you may even feel exposed or scared about something. Losing one's teeth is another common dream which can mean the loss of power or a fear of getting old. And last but not least, if you dream that you are being killed it means that you are scared of someone or feel they have some kind of hold over you, or you are worried about something. It could also indicate that you are holding onto something from the past that needs 'killing off'.

E is for Esoteric

"Moonlight floods the whole sky from horizon to horizon; how much it can fill your room depends on its windows."

—RUMI

This is a word that seems to be popping up more and more lately. Even in spirituality there seem to be buzz words or titles for things that have been around for centuries. Basically it means leading a spiritual life and the belief that we come here with nothing in terms of material gain. Once born, as we grow, we learn what we have to in our Earthly bodies and then return to the spirit world without any of our Earthly possessions. All we take back to the spirit world are the lessons we have learned here on Earth. The phrase 'You can't take it with you when you go' is very true, so live your life to the full – you only have once chance at it!

F is for Fairy

"Fairies are invisible and inaudible like angels but their magic sparkles in nature."

—LYNN HOLLAND

Although I have never had the pleasure personally, I am hearing more and more stories about people who have met one of the little people. I love to see pictures of them in books and I make up stories about them when telling my granddaughter a bed-time story. Stories just pop into my head so I never read out of a book to her. We even have regular characters that return to have different magical adventures. There is one common theme - there always seems to be a fairy in the story somewhere! So maybe on a sub-conscious level they are working with me already.

I recently wrote a meditation in which a fairy appears; I read out the guided meditation to my Soul Magic Class. After the meditation I asked for feedback as usual but what was consistent with each person was that they all 'saw' the fairy as clear as day. I asked that the fairy gave them a word or a message for them to bring back to consciousness, and each message or word was significant even though each person didn't realise it at the time. So there really could be a magical land at the bottom of your garden just out of reach of curious eyes, unless they want you to see them of course!

F is for Frequently Asked Questions

"Judge a man by his questions rather than his answers."

—VOLTAIRE

During my work as a medium and healer, I get asked many questions and some of them more than others. Here is a selection of the more frequent.

How did you get the job as co-host on Rescue Mediums?

I was working for the police when I went along for an audition to be Jackie's new partner on the show. I thought, 'Why not?' It would be excellent experience and a lot of fun. In the audition, I had to open up to spirit and communicate with whoever came through. A wonderful lady in spirit came through with clarity and when I described her to Jackie it turned out to be someone very close to her. I felt totally relaxed in the audition and I couldn't believe it when a few weeks later I was told that the W Network had chosen me as Jackie's new partner in the show.

Is the whole show filmed in Canada or is some of it in the UK?

All the filming is done in Canada which is a country I had never been to before, as I didn't have specific links to Canada at that time. We have a fabulous crew who welcomed me into their fold, and I had a lovely surprise last year when I met my cousin Stuart and his family who live just outside Toronto. I hadn't seen Stuart for over thirty years so it was quite an emotional reunion! Canadian people are so warm, friendly and welcoming and I have friends in the country who are always inviting me to stay.

Is there a difference between being psychic and being a medium?

I am a clairvoyant medium which means that I can see what others cannot through my third eye, which is an intuitive sight where I can see images similar to a photographic print from my inner mind. As a medium I can communicate with spirit and also receive messages from my spirit guides. I can also hear sounds that other people can't hear, which is known as clairaudience, and I can sense spirit around me which is known as clairsentience where I sometimes pick up on any physical pain they encountered when on Earth, especially when I'm doing rescue work.

Have you ever passed on bad news to a client?

It depends what you deem to be bad news. With experience you learn how to convey information to the client that would, in the long term, help them. For example, if my spirit guide said that the person had bad stomach pains and they hadn't been to the doctor, then I would diplomatically suggest they speak to their GP to put their mind at rest. This is something that could save someone's life so I don't see it as bad news as such. Obviously I have a code of conduct to uphold and I use my professionalism, empathy and discretion at all times when relaying information to clients. Most of the messages I receive are from loved ones in spirit who are around that person as a protective measure, so if the person is going through an emotional time, for example, it is comforting for them to know that their loved one is around them helping to guide them forward to a more enlightening future.

Can you see into the future?

I am often asked to give people the lottery numbers for that week and when I'm asked this question it proves to me that some people can be very naive about what mediumship is all about. If that was all there was to it, it would demean my psychic abilities and I certainly wouldn't see it as a gift. It's a constant awareness, but when developed in the right way you learn with experience how to 'tune in' and 'tune out'. Another way of putting it is 'opening up' and 'closing down' - opening one's chakras to be able to communicate with the spirit world. However, on occasion I do get information for someone without consciously 'tuning in' and of course I have to pass that information on as it's not mine to keep.

What has scared you the most on the Rescue Mediums TV show?

Seeing my psychic art on the show for the first time! Seriously though, one of the scariest episodes in Season Four was in a pub. The spirit was very aggressive. As we walked around the building he told us to "Get out" and that he didn't like women. I felt him pinch me and it made me jump; as I mentioned this to Jackie, her head jolted backwards as he head-butted her. I bet there are not many people around who have been head-butted by a ghost! He continued taunting us by swearing and putting physical conditions on us.

We had decided to do the rescue in the basement which was dark, cold and depressing. As we sat down he was rocking the table and I felt him pull me back so hard I nearly fell off my chair. The activity was getting stronger so without a moment to lose we closed our eyes and started to bring in the light. After I while I sensed that something wasn't right as it had gone deathly quiet, and my heart thumped loudly as I looked over to Jackie. Her face had changed and she was shaking with anger. All of a sudden she thumped the table so hard that it moved and I screamed with fright. As he had a hold over Jackie I had to do something so I asked him his name - "David" was his reply. He said he was looking for someone as he wanted revenge and each time he thought of this he got angrier and angrier. He was taking all Jackie's energy and I called to her but she couldn't reply. If I'm honest I wanted to run out of that basement and never look back, but that's the coward's way out so I decided to try a little 'counselling'. I asked David to think of a lovely memory, a time when he was truly happy, and when I asked where he was he spoke through Jackie telling me that he was a boy again playing in the open air with his dog. Jackie's face had gone softer and I knew he wasn't so angry now, so I asked who he would like to see more than anyone in the world and he replied "Mom". He had calmed down and seemed to be enjoying his childhood memories so I called his Mom forward to guide him over to the light. I felt a shift of energy as I saw the light come down and there was a lady waiting for him. He turned and saw his mother and I saw Jackie's face light up as mother and son were reunited. As David walked into the light with his mother by his side he was a little boy again and I saw tears rolling down Jackie's face. This was a strong spirit and we were both relieved when he went through to the light with his mother by his side. We closed the door, filled the rest of the building with light and both of us felt the heaviness in the room disappear.

Are you religious? What are your beliefs?

I believe in God, and the celestial realms. I work closely with the angels to help to bring their love and serenity into the lives of others. I also believe in revering the wonders of Mother Earth in all her beauty. Nature to me is the pinnacle of everything I stand for; I love the animals, flowers, plants, trees, birds and each of our four seasons. Everyone is unique and of course people will have different religious beliefs. I feel that as long as everyone is happy, it doesn't matter what their religion is (or not, as the case may be). The key to a peaceful and fulfilled life is being happy and content from within. I feel that spirituality as a whole is linked, whether it's from a religious or mediumistic aspect. Both help to bring comfort to the lost and lonely and to those whose loved ones have moved on to the next world.

How can I tell if I have psychic abilities?

Are you sensitive to the point of feeling you are like a sponge, soaking up other people's emotions? Do you have strong intuition or gut feeling? Do you sense when something is about to happen or when the `phone is going to ring? Do you have premonitions about the future? Do lights go up and down in the house when you are around? Do you feel that you often live in a world of your own and that you feel different but can't explain why? If you have answered "Yes" to any of these questions then you are probably psychic and need to ground yourself every day and, if possible, join your local Spiritualist church so you can develop your psychic abilities.

Do my loved ones in spirit know that I have got married, or had a baby, or got a new job, etcetera?

In a word, yes, they do, as when our loved ones pass to spirit their souls live on. If you want validation of this, ask your loved one to leave you a sign that they are around you. This will either be something that was personal to both of you or they will leave a feather for you in an unusual place. One of the signs that our loved ones send us is birds, so if you are thinking about them as a robin flies into the garden, be assured it's a message from the spirit world that they are happy and at peace. When people come to me for a reading they worry that their loved ones have missed out on events in their lives and although they are not there in body, they are certainly there in spirit. I have given so many messages to clients that have confirmed that their loved one has been around them during an exciting event in their life. You may not be able to see them, but they are there, surrounding you with their love and light.

How do you deal with sceptics?

Over the years I have met people who have either sneered at what I do or tried their best to 'trip me up'. However, they get a shock when I give them messages from spirit that are personal to them and the information is often something they have never shared with anyone else. The usual retort I receive is "How do you know that?" which is often accompanied by a look of shock and horror on their faces. In general, I never force my beliefs on others and in some respects I am fairly quiet about the work I do. Only when the conversation opens up to psychic abilities or spirituality as a whole do I share my love of all things spiritual.

Who has been your role model or mentor?

My first mentor is my friend Pam, although if she were reading this she would be very surprised that I have included her as one of my mentors, which says it all about why she deserves to get a mention! She is extremely spiritual and helped me through the dark days by introducing me to Reiki, taking me along to one of her psychic circles and recommending spiritual and self-help books to read. We met at school but weren't close friends as we were in different classes. A few years later I was on a bus and she got on with her son Paul who was a toddler at the time. We got chatting and realised that we lived near one another with our respective partners so we agreed to meet up one evening a week when our husbands were at work.

AN ABC OF SPIRITUALITY

We have remained close friends ever since and I know that Pam will always be there for me, as I am for her.

My other mentor is, of course, Jackie who is my partner on the show Rescue Mediums. She was my wonderful Psychic Development teacher and helped me to develop my gift in a safe environment giving me support throughout my training. She put me at my ease when I started working with her as co-host on the Rescue Mediums show and you only have to look at some of the photographs taken during filming to see what fun we had.

Another person who has helped me whilst developing my gift is Joey Martinez who lives in Gibraltar. When attending one of his weekend workshops entitled Working With Higher Energies, he came over and said he could see my natural abilities and that I shouldn't 'try too hard'. I heeded his advice as they were such wise words which I now share with others.

Everyone thinks that to be psychic or a medium, you have to put so much energy and thought into it. Well you don't! It is a natural gift that has been bestowed on you, so just enjoy it! I am still in touch with Joey and his family and a few years ago he came over to the UK and I attuned him to become a Reiki Master. I love going to Gibraltar and seeing him and his lovely wife Rose as well as feeling the wonderful energies around such a beautiful place steeped in history.

What happens behind the scenes on the Rescue Mediums show?

A lot happens behind the scenes. We have a fabulous crew and we really are like one big happy family. The first part of filming is where Jackie and I read our premonitions out to each other and share what we have drawn through the means of psychic art. It is usual for people to double up laughing at some of my pictures! As I have said before, I am no artist but the clues are there as we find out later on when doing our 'walkabout' or when doing the 'rescue'.

During this initial part of filming we wear our own clothes. Our crew consists of two cameramen, a sound technician, production manager, production assistant, a technical assistant, our head of research Edna, Jackie and I as co-hosts of the show, and our producer Michael Lamport and director Gregory Shepherd. The crew have to arrive early to set up their equipment and the sound guy has to 'mike up' us two ladies. Once everyone is in position, the crew do a couple of sound checks and we are ready to roll.

Once everyone is happy and the filming has finished, Michael, Edna and the rest of the crew have to go to the location (the haunted property). Jackie and I will change into our 'show clothes' and we usually have a bit of lunch with our director Gregory while the others set up their equipment at the location and film the homeowners, who share their experiences such as explaining how paranormal phenomena have been affecting them, what exactly has been happening in the property and what they have seen, felt or heard. Jackie and I never know where we are going or anything about the homeowners or what they have been going through, so when Gregory receives the call from Michael that we can travel to the location, it is literally 'a mystery tour' and we both love this part of the show. When we arrive at the property we get quite excited as we can see from our premonitions which clues have already been identified.

For example we may have written down cows, sheep and horses and Greg will pull up in front of a farm! Our whole crew know to keep everything secret from us and they have got it down to a fine art. When we get out of the car, our sound guy comes out to 'mike' us up again for the initial bit of filming with the homeowners. We are then filmed knocking at the door and meeting the homeowners who lead us into the room where the crew have set up their equipment. It can be a revelation even at this early stage because we can often see some of our premonition clues in the room.

We sit down with the members of the family and read our premonitions out to them and show them our psychic art. They are not allowed to give us any information but can say 'Yes' or 'No' or nod in agreement if we have touched on something that has been happening in the property. I know this is hard for them but it is imperative that we find out for ourselves what has been happening to maintain the credibility of the show. When this part of the show has been filmed, the homeowners leave the property and the crew set up their equipment in readiness for Jackie and me to do our 'walkabout'.

This part of the show entails us walking around the property including the outside perimeter so we can gather more clues along the way which we discuss as well as saying how each of us feels, what we see and if we encounter anything that may help us in our psychic investigation. We 'invite' the spirits to communicate with us so we can try to build up a picture of who is haunting the property and why. Everything we say on film at this point is written down by hand by Edna. When we have looked outside and been in every room in the house, we leave and get something to eat before travelling back to our accommodation in Toronto.

The next day involves the filming of 'the arrival'. For those of you who watch the show, you will have seen Jackie and me arriving in all sorts of weird and wonderful modes of transport and some of my favourite ones are snow shoes, a tractor, motorbike and sidecar, horse and trap, and a golf cart. The ones that gave me the willies were the hearse and a wood cart that was so high we had to walk up a ladder with nothing to hold onto, and I had to be lifted into the cart as it was so deep. I very nearly refused to do this one as I don't like ladders and I couldn't stop shaking, but I persevered. I couldn't let the side down, could I? I'm glad I did it as it looks hilarious on the episode, but my legs were shaking for ages afterwards.

Once the filming of the arrival has been done, it is time for us to get a bite to eat before we start our rescue. The film crew set all their equipment up in the house and we speak to our director to inform him of the room we feel we should start in when we begin our rescue. We usually come to this conclusion from the information we have picked up during the walkabout and it could be that it is where we both felt the presence of the spirit, or it could be something that both of us have in our premonitions. On other occasions it will be the map or area I have drawn in my psychic art which is a clue as to where we need to be to do the rescue.

Each and every clue or eventuality is discussed at length between us so we agree on the right area. The cameramen set up their cameras, Jackie and I are 'miked up' and everyone else gets into position. It is crucial that the crew remain silent because if anyone moves or makes a noise it could deter the spirit or break the communication between Jackie and me and the spirit. The first thing we do once we are settled in the relevant area is to send white light throughout the house. If we are in one of the bedrooms we start at the bottom of the building from the basement and bring the light up and around each room and crevice in the house. The spirit will move within the light and as they do so we start to communicate with them by receiving messages through images or hearing names and so forth. This is a critical time in the investigation and we have to literally give it our all. We never know who we are encountering and we could be dealing with something very nasty so it takes all our concentration and nerve.

We both meditate and talk to our respective spirit guides who help us as we make contact with the spirits. It is usual in a lot of cases that one of us is 'overshadowed'. This means that the spirit will come so close that they are literally 'in our face' and we can sometimes take on their persona which can be extremely frightening, but we must keep our nerve at all times. On one occasion we were sitting on a bed trying to make contact with the spirit. Everything was quiet – too quiet – and when I looked over at Jackie it was evident that the spirit had taken a tight hold. I wasn't prepared at all for what I saw, as Jackie looked hideous (sorry, Jackie!). She was drooling and slavering, making spitting noises through her teeth and an appalling animal-type growl from deep within her throat. Her face was bright red and twisted and she couldn't speak coherently to me; all I heard were delirious mumblings and I felt clammy and sick to the pit of my stomach and I actually screamed out with fright. I'd never seen such visible overshadowing before and I was scared out of my wits. However, I had to summon all my strength to help Jackie by communicating with the spirit and, after what seemed like forever, we managed to send him over to the light. Once she'd composed herself I shouted, "Please don't ever do that again, you frightened me to death, you looked horrible!" Not that she had any say in the matter. When a spirit connects with us that strongly it takes an enormous amount of energy, courage and strength to contain them and send them to the light. It all boils down to trusting each other implicitly and to teamwork.

During a rescue I can feel my spirit guides close by my side and I know that I am also protected by the angels. Spirit rescue work can be extremely dangerous and we couldn't perform our psychic investigation and the rescue without our wonderful helpers being by our side. Once we start to receive information from the spirit we ask someone to come forward for them and in most instances it is a family member from the 'other side'.

This can be very rewarding and in a lot of cases very emotional as we can see them at last meeting up with their loved ones when they are guided over to the light. Once they have gone, we discuss what happened between ourselves and ask for some water as we can feel dehydrated, or for tissues if it has been an emotional rescue.

Our show lasts for twenty-two minutes when it airs on television but the reality is that we can spend hours communicating with the spirit and trying to send them to the light; so by the time all of us have packed up and gone to our respective homes it is often extremely late when we get back to Toronto and I always feel exhausted and ready for my bed.

The following day is 'research day' when Edna has to pull together all the information that Jackie and I have given during the investigation and she will often go to speak to historians in the area to look through archived records and try to find out who is haunting the property. Edna has a very difficult job to do which is why Jackie and I try to get as much information as we can during the rescue such as names, dates, events and so on, so she can pinpoint exactly who it was we sent to the light and obtain the relevant historical facts so that we can tell the story and share the independent research at our Show and Tell.

On the last day of filming, Jackie and I are up very early and we meet Edna so we can write up everything about the history of the person we have rescued including their family tree and birth and death certificates, which will tell the whole story of their lives and why they were haunting the house. The information has to be accurate, detailed and in chronological order. It takes a lot of concentration and hard work but it's worth it when we see the reaction of the homeowners. Once we have all our documents, photographs and information ready, we put them with our relevant psychic drawings and premonitions and hand them over to Edna. She makes us up a folder each containing the documents which she passes to us at the location. We have a bit of lunch and Jackie and I get changed into a different set of clothes. Edna will then take us to the homeowners' property where our crew have already set up their equipment in readiness for us to film the Show and Tell.

This part of the show involves us sitting down with the homeowners and they are allowed to tell us everything that has been going on in their home or place of work. We then share what we found when conducting our psychic investigation and what happened during the rescue. There are usually a few tears during this part of the show which can be a mixture of relief and happiness as the homeowners feel that they have finally got their home back and they can get on with their lives again, confirming that their home feels 'lighter'. Other comments made are that members of the family have got their personalities back, there is no feeling of depression anymore, and one lovely lady said that for her and husband, "The torment and fear are no longer hanging over us and that is something so profound that we'll never forget and always hold very dear to our hearts." Both Jackie and I enjoy this part of the show immensely as we find out what the homeowners have been experiencing and we tell them exactly what we found, which makes for very interesting viewing. It can also be extremely rewarding for us when we hear how accurate we have been with our premonitions and psychic art. I truly love my job!

When the filming has finished, Jackie and I say our goodbyes to the homeowners. On each episode you can see us hugging them and walking down the path and along the street looking back at them, waving. The crew then put all the equipment back into the van and Jackie and I are driven to a local area where we will film our 'Cheers'.

What do you personally go through before, during and after a rescue?

Before a rescue, I ground myself and envelop myself in psychic protection with white light, my cloak and the mirrors. I often feel quite apprehensive at this stage as I don't know what we are going to come up against, especially if during the walkabout there has been minimal or no contact with the spirit. It is hard to generalise what I go through during the rescue as each one is different. But, as an example, if we are dealing with a nasty spirit I am often shown horrendous images or snippets of the spirit's life – usually parts of it that are related to why they didn't go to the light. This can be anything from feeling angry or hurt by another person, feeling alone or unwanted or just being downright evil. I can pick up on their emotions whether sad or angry, and they often put physical conditions onto me. On one occasion I felt extremely dizzy and fell to the floor; I had to crawl around on all fours for a while as I felt too weak to stand up. I have also fainted a few times which can be embarrassing. When I am overshadowed I feel overwhelming emotions and can often feel my face or body shape changing. I remember during one investigation that my voice changed and went very deep as the male spirit overshadowed me, although this doesn't happen very often, thank goodness!

Another example of a spirit getting 'physical' is when a scratch appeared on my neck that wasn't there before, and when Jackie saw blood dripping down my face. It is a relief when we finally make contact and through sheer teamwork we manage to send the spirit to the light. Once this has happened we can feel the room change and the only way I can explain this is that everything feels warmer, lighter and as if a big weight has been lifted and the home has got its soul back. Sometimes there can be residual energy left in the property so I will go round to each room and 'draw' Reiki symbols on the walls to help give it a lift. Both of us will also give the homeowners advice about which crystals to place in the property and how to smudge a room.

After each rescue we feel literally drained to the point of sheer exhaustion but it is such a rewarding time knowing we have helped the spirit as well as our homeowners. I always look forward to our 'Cheers'!

Why do spirits suddenly start haunting a place?

There could be a number of reasons why a spirit haunts a property, far too many to mention within this book. However, as an example, it could be links to the land rather than the property itself or it could be an attachment to a person in the family if they have dabbled with an ouija board or similar. If it is the house then it could be a former owner, or just that someone in the home is psychic; if they have visited somewhere that the spirit has inhabited, the spirit could have been attracted to the light that the person is shining out, and followed them home.

How has your work affected the people you have helped? How have their lives changed because of what you do?

When you watch the show you can see the gratitude that our homeowners convey during our Show and Tell. These poor people have literally been to hell and back with what they have experienced, so it is such a relief for them to enjoy their homes and family once again. Very often people have felt extremely ill or depressed due to activity in the home and it's like a great weight has been lifted off their shoulders once the spirit has gone to the light. They will often say to us that they felt a difference straight away although in rare cases it can take a while before the residual energy dissipates. Properties hold negative energy and when there is a nasty spirit or entity it literally seeps through the walls of the property.

In the case of the shape-shifter, the family 'escaped' from their home as they couldn't stand living in it any more. Their daughter had changed personality from a sweet girl into an angry person that they didn't recognise, and they knew it was the influence of the spirit that was making her like this. Their home felt cold and unwelcome and in order to keep their family together they left the property, but I am happy to say that once we had done our rescue they returned and said what a different place it felt. Once again they knew they would be happy and safe in their beautiful home.

A lot of our homeowners still keep in touch and tell us how they are getting on with their lives and have new jobs, met new friends, and one lady now has her own successful esoteric shop selling beautiful crystals, angel figurines and books.

How long does a rescue take?

My answer to this is, "How long is a piece of string?" As most of you who watch the show will realise, the rescue doesn't take the 10 or 15 minutes which is usually the part that is shown on air. Unfortunately, sometimes the editors even have to take out a rescue in its entirety. The reason for this is that we often have more than one rescue in a property and there isn't always the time to show each one. Both Jackie and I get disappointed sometimes when both rescues are not shown as we know what hard work has gone into sending the wayward spirit to the light, and we feel that viewers would want to share in that experience. However, we understand that the main thing is that the spirit has gone to their loved ones on the other side and the homeowners are now 'spirit free'.

I couldn't say exactly how long a rescue takes as each one is different but it can literally take hours as we have to communicate with the spirit and coax them in a lot of cases to go towards the light. We have had a case of one spirit whom we felt was nearly over, and then he turned his back on the light and ran back which was very frustrating. In cases like this, it takes all our energy and willpower to be able to stay calm and professional and eventually guide them over.

What is a typical day like for you?

I am a normal everyday person and, yes, I do have an incredible gift, but my day is probably not dissimilar to yours. I get up, shower, dress, put my make-up on, have a cup of tea and take the dog for a walk, having a light breakfast on my return. I will pick up my emails and tweets. If I have readings for that day I prepare my meditation room, creating the right ambience for my clients such as cleaning around, changing old tea lights for new, getting out my angel and Tarot cards. Then I will 'open up' and talk to my guides whilst meditating, often creating a 'prediction list' which I know will be for my clients as part of their reading.

I will answer telephone calls, organise workshops, ring people back as necessary and update my website. Evenings are spent with my husband but lately this hasn't happened much as I have been working on my book, so he really deserves a medal as he has become a 'book widower'! I organise my spiritual practice around my 'day job' and at present it is working out really well. I like to be organised and I couldn't go anywhere without my trusted diary; how people manage without one I really don't know. People laugh at me because it seems so old-fashioned these days to carry a diary around with you, but I may get 'with the times' if Father Christmas brings me an iPad. I've dropped enough hints to my husband…

What would I expect if I came for a reading with you?

My main concern is that you feel comfortable and are open to the messages I am about to give you, so I always put my clients at ease by explaining about what to expect during their reading. It will be just like having a chat, only I will be picking up messages from spirit, as well as giving you names and information either around you now that you will recognise, or for the future. I recommend that clients write this information down because once I'm 'on a roll' you won't remember everything I have said. My readings are unique in that I do get very unusual information and I often receive something from spirit that the client has never told anyone before. That is why I do what I do, as they cannot ask for more succinct confirmation from the afterlife. I always finish my readings with psychic Tarot and angel cards, which often give the person the same as I have conveyed during the spiritual part of the reading, but with more clarification.

I did one reading recently where the lady's grandfather came through and he gave her his name and information around the family. However, she asked me if I would speak to him and ask him a direct question which was, "What did you make by hand when I was a child that intrigued me?" So I asked the male spirit the question and I was shown a tiny house. I told my client what I could see and I knew there was something very unusual about it as it wasn't a dolls' house. She confirmed that he used to make little houses out of matchsticks and they used to be displayed in building societies when she was a child. She then asked me to ask him to show me what used to drive him mad about her when she was little, and he showed me a little girl sitting at a piano and she confirmed this also.

At one of the Mind Body and Spirit fairs recently a gentleman who had booked in with me sat down for his reading and said when he looked at the leaflet advertising the event that my face seemed to glow, so he knew he had to come to me. I started off the reading by saying I was being given 'Morocco' and he nearly fell off his chair. He said they had just booked a holiday that week to go to Morocco, and as I confirmed further events in his life and guidance for the future he said he knew why he had to come to me for his reading. He thoroughly enjoyed the occasion and he has passed my name on to others who have since been to see me for clairvoyant readings.

F is also for Fun!

"As long as you're having fun, that's the key. The moment it becomes a grind, it's over."

—BARRY GIBB

A favourite quote of mine is: 'Angels can fly as they take themselves lightly'. Sometimes we get so caught up in either our own problems or the problems of others that we forget how to have fun. When was the last time you had a really good laugh? Or did something that you truly love? Be creative – paint, draw, sing, dance or anything else that lights up your soul. Get in touch with friends and go out and have a great evening putting the world to rights, or go to the cinema to watch an uplifting film. When you are having fun, endorphins in the body are released which gives you that 'feel good factor'. Once fun kicks in, you realise that you haven't worried or thought about anything negative during the time you are enjoying yourself, so do it more often. You deserve it.

G is for Ghosts

"The law is pressed by unseen feet, and ghosts return gently at twilight, gently go at dawn, the sad intangible who greave and yearn."

—T S ELLIOTT, TO WALTER DE LA MARE

I prefer the word spirits as opposed to ghosts. Sometimes there are spirits that appear nasty but most of them are confused and are only trying to attract someone's attention so they can be sent to the light and meet their loved ones once again. However, when there is a spirit attachment it can be a horrific experience for the person involved and it can only be removed by someone in my profession who has the relevant experience and know-how. Never, ever, try to get rid of an attachment yourself as you could be asking for trouble. Here are some true life 'ghost stories'.

Anna (name changed)

"A very interesting (but long) case is about an attachment I had; I only got rid of him a few months back with the help of a shaman in Glastonbury. He would visit me in dreams and try to astral rape me. My close friends were visited by him or were even receiving messages by my guides to warn of him. His contempt for women has left me with some female issues. This entity attached to my Mum who is a nurse at the hospital when he passed on. Then through her it attached to me. He would visit my partner in his dreams and it took my spirit guide, a nun, to visit some of my sensitive friends warning them. Sometimes he would overpower me when my auric field was low and make me drink more, etcetera, then I would blackout and he would take over. People who saw this would see me arguing in the mirror beforehand."

Barbara

"It was the summer of 1976 and my brother and his wife, who live in South-port, Lancashire, had recently moved house after having their first child. They had invited me and my boyfriend to stay over for the weekend to see the house and have an evening out. My brother also invited his friend Paul who was a chemist and his girlfriend who was a nurse. We were going to see Kenny Ball and his Jazzmen who were to perform in a marquee in Formby. We had a great evening out; the weather had been perfect for such an event. Helen, my brother's new daughter, was safely tucked up in her cot at home with a babysitter looking after her. We were all level-headed people in the car – a dentist and his wife, a gardener, myself a civil servant, a chemist and a nurse. None of us had had a drink as it wasn't that type of event. So there we were, the six of us driving home to Southport in the car.

"My brother had an old maroon Bentley at the time which was fabu-lous for going on picnics, etcetera. I was sitting next to my brother who was driving and his wife was next to the passenger door. In the back was my boyfriend, the chemist and the nurse. It was now dark and as we drove down the bypass, my brother said to me, "Did you see that?" and I said, "What?" He said he'd just seen something or someone that was lit up by the car headlights – they were all in white and they seemed to be like a mummy. He was really shocked and we told him to go back so we could see what he was talking about; he thought that maybe someone had had an accident or he hadn't seen what he actually thought he'd seen. So we went round the roundabout and retraced our journey back again. He drove slowly up the bypass and said, "There it is!" We all saw it then – the image was picked up by the car headlights and we drew closer and closer to try to make it out. It looked like a mummy with bandages hanging from it and as he slowed down even further it walked up the grass verge towards the car with its arms held out to us as if pleading for help. Both Sue, my brother's girlfriend, and I were hysterical, trying to lock the car door and all of us were shouting to my brother to drive off fast – which he did, quickly!

"When we got home my brother took the babysitter back home to Formby and my boyfriend went with him. Unbeknown to us, after dropping the babysitter off at home they went down the bypass again and got out of the car to check the hedges in the area to ensure no-one was injured e.g. a motorbike or a car accident. They found nothing, so they reported it to the local police station just in case someone was lying injured somewhere. They then called the RAF base on the bypass and explained what we had all seen. The RAF said they would check the area and contact them later. They telephoned my brother that evening and said they had found nothing. They also said not to worry as they have had so many weird and unexplained sightings reported to them in the area surrounding the airbase. It is an old base and I can only explain what we saw as a pilot who was covered in flameproof bandages (which they wore in war times) who had probably crashed (Second World War?) and was staggering about. That's the only way I can describe it... and we all saw it... so who really knows who it was?

"That evening none of us slept. Paul (the chemist) and his wife went home. My boyfriend and I stayed over at my brother's house. They had only just moved into the property so there were no carpets or decorating done and all night we could hear loud tapping noises which was unnerving especially after the incident we had experienced. I never left the bedroom! In the morning my brother and Sue said they had been unnerved by the same unexplained noises. We went home the next day and about a week later my brother contacted me. The situation on the bypass was still a mystery, but the loud tapping in the house had been solved. It was Helen, my baby niece tapping her head on the headboard of the cot which, as there were no carpets, was echoing through the house!"

Pip

When doing my hair one day, Pip my hairdresser told me about a 'hair-raising' experience in her house when she was younger and I asked if I could include it in my book. Here is what happened.

When Pip was a child and living at home with her sister and mother, their neighbour passed away suddenly from cancer leaving a single father on his own with two boys to look after. As he needed to work to provide for his family and was doing shift-work, Pip's Mum wanted to help in any way she could; so she said she would look after the boys while their father was on nights. The eldest boy had a bed in Pip's room and the youngest child who at nine years old was the same age as Pip's sister Abbey, shared her room. In Pip's words, "He was a strange child who was freakishly clever." However, they obviously felt so sorry for the boys with their mother dying so suddenly that they wanted to do what they could to help. The first sign that something was wrong was a couple of nights later, when Abbey had a horrific nightmare – sitting bolt upright in bed screaming at the top of her voice. Her eyes were open and she screamed and screamed. She would then get up in the night and stand by either Pip's bedroom door or her Mum's bedroom door and carry on screaming. This carried on, but things got much worse.

The family had palm crosses dotted through the house, and one morning when they got up they found all of the crosses stacked together. In usual fashion when something like this happens, the family were blaming each other; but no-one owned up to doing this and they all swore blind that they hadn't moved them. A few days later Pip woke up to find her rug of the Last Supper rolled up in the corner of her room. She asked her Mum and Abbey why they had done this, but neither of them owned up to it. All the while Abbey's night terrors got worse and worse, so her mother called in a priest to bless Abbey's room and hopefully find out what was causing all the problems.

The priest came and did as he had been asked; but when he came out of Abbey's room he said that there was a very dark and negative feeling around the china clown doll that hung on the end of Abbey's bed.

Earlier that week, Pip had had a nightmare about the china clown which they told the priest about, and he told the family to get rid of it as quickly as possible. After the priest had gone, the girls' mother went into Abbey's room to pray but felt extremely scared and anxious and decided to clear out the room. As she was dusting under the spare bed in which the young boy from next door had been sleeping she found some books. As she looked through them, she was shocked to find that the majority of them were about how to summon up negative and dark energies – in other words, it was obvious that he had been practising with 'the dark arts' and she realised that he had 'invited' in something very negative which had taken possession of the china clown. Without further ado, she did as the priest had advised and straight away she gave the doll to the bin men to take away.

That night, Abbey slept through the night with no night terrors for the first time in ages. Needless to say, they didn't invite the boys to stay any more in their home, and the room felt extremely peaceful and inviting again. As you can imagine, Pip doesn't like clowns in any shape way or form. But it's hardly surprising, is it?

Nick

"Every year at Easter, my two children Samantha and Louise who were very young at the time used to visit my mother and step-father's home in Birkby near Huddersfield in West Yorkshire for the Easter break for a week. My parents' home was a fairly new property built out of millstone grit but in a modern style. It had four bedrooms, a large through lounge and a separate dining room. The kitchen was large too with a table and a couple of chairs in it at one end where my parents used to eat their breakfast. I think the house was built in the grounds of an old Victorian property which was owned by the owner of a woollen mill; the house had extensive grounds, a bit like a stately home but on a smaller scale, the grounds of which were sold off for a housing development. The house still remains and is called Rosehill.

"For several years and on numerous occasions my mother used to joke that her house had a ghost which she used to call Charlie, apparently after an old man who was the head gardener for Rosehill for many years. The reason my mother thought there was a presence in the house was that before she went to bed she would place items, particularly in the dining room on the table or on the sideboard, and when she came down in the morning they had been moved by Charlie and she would find them elsewhere in the house. These occurrences could possibly be explained by forgetfulness or misplacement of the items, or perhaps she had had a tipple the night before; however it did seem to happen quite a lot!

"On one particular occasion things happened which could not be explained. The story I am about to tell you was corroborated by my step-father who was a smart, well-dressed, retired businessman who always wore a tie and suit trousers at home and a suit and tie for work. He was an honest man with scruples and was not the sort of person to make things up or tell lies. You get my drift! My mother telephoned on this particular occasion to finalise the arrangements to take my daughters over to their house to stay for the Easter week, but during the conversation she said, 'I have something to tell you that has happened in the house. But don't tell the girls as it may frighten them and put them off coming to the house.'

"She said that one morning she and my step-father had gone downstairs into the kitchen to have breakfast. My step-father had sat at the kitchen table whilst my mother put two rashers of bacon and two fried eggs into a frying pan on top of the stove and turned it on. As my mother's hob was of the old electric type and not halogen it took quite some time to get hot, so she moved away from the stove, presumably to get the plates and utensils ready. Whilst she was away from the stove both she and my step-father observed a peculiar happening. All of a sudden, one single rasher of bacon rose into the air from the frying pan, moved to one side and dropped onto the kitchen floor. The second rasher of bacon then rose from the pan and did exactly the same thing, followed by each egg in turn which smashed on contact with the floor.

"I took the girls over to my mother's house without telling them what my mother had told me. I questioned my step-father about the occurrence and he told me that if he had not seen it with his own eyes he would never have believed it. My mother, of course, laughed it off saying it must have been 'Charlie' and to date the incident has never been explained."

Stephen

Geordie Stephen says "Wayay man!" when he remembers what happened on his most frightening ghost hunt ever…

"I had booked in to Borthwick Castle in the Scottish Borders on Hallowe'en for the Red Room, which is the most haunted room in the castle, as I needed research for a book I was writing at the time. On arrival I made a beeline for the guest-book to the bemusement of the German couple in Reception at the time. The reason I do this is because it's where people write whether they have had any spooky experiences and I wanted to see what they had said.

"I decided to spend a solo vigil in the Mary Queen of Scots room instead. I'd had a 'run in' with Mary on a previous occasion and on this particular evening I walked into the room and shone my torch on a painting on the wall of Mary, thinking to myself that she was better looking than I had envisaged her. Maybe this wasn't the best thought I'd ever had!

"I noticed there was a large four-poster bed in the room but I chose to sit where Mary used to put her make-up on; I knew this because I'd been on the tour previously and had been told that, because this area was the brightest in the castle, this was where she used to sit. Whilst sitting there, I asked the spirit world to let me know if there was anyone in the room, in particular Mary. I asked if she could give me a sign of her presence by knocking once for 'Yes' and at that point there was a knock in the far corner of the room by the door. I asked her to repeat this as I needed validation that it was Mary communicating with me. She obliged by knocking once again and, although she'd done as I had asked, I still needed proof as I thought it may just have been natural noises such as radiators knocking or the room settling. I decided to go one step further, so I asked her out loud if she was happy with an English guy being in her room and asked her to knock once for 'Yes' and twice for 'No'. The knock when it came seemed much closer this time and seemed to indicate that she was moving closer to me, so and I asked her to verify this. She knocked once for 'Yes'! I then asked if I was sitting where she used to sit when putting her make-up on. Again when she knocked once it was nearer still and I could feel my heart pounding, as I knew I only had a couple of questions left before she would be standing in front of me and I didn't want to put myself in the position of being overshadowed whilst being on my own. I had to ask again if she was comfortable with an English guy being in her comfort zone when she lived here, and there were then two knocks for 'No'! By this time I knew I had to be very canny on what would possibly be my next and final question!

"I started gathering all my personal belongings together and I asked her, 'Do you want me to stay or leave?' I jumped with a start when I heard an almighty cracking sound which made me jump out of my skin and I couldn't believe what I saw. The wood on the four-poster bed was cracked. It was obvious that Mary Queen of Scots was definitely not happy that an English guy was in her bedroom so I made a hasty retreat and scarpered out of the room."

Bill

"Twenty-five years ago I met a woman whom I fell in love with and we began dating and were getting pretty serious about each other. At least, it seemed that way to me at the time. Things were going well until I began to notice that she began drinking more and more. I complained about it which led to an argument, and we parted ways. Later, I tried to reconcile with her but by then she had moved on and had met someone new.

"It took me a while to pick up the pieces, but eventually I did and met another person. At this time, my previous girlfriend Sam (name changed) began contacting me again. She told me that she was frequenting a particular bar that I often went to and asked why I didn't go down there as much, because she hadn't seen me around for ages. I went to the bar to meet her and we went out the once but I didn't work out.

"A few months later I saw her again at the same bar with her new boyfriend and she appeared to be drunk. She came over to talk to me and I could see that she had been crying although she didn't explain the reason why. Eventually her boyfriend carried her out of the pub and that was the last I saw of her. I have to admit I was upset and I was worried about her. In fact, the whole incident unnerved me and although life went on I never forgot her.

"Several years later I found myself with a failed marriage, early retirement due to ill-health and as a single parent raising two teenagers. Life hadn't been kind to me but I carried on and tried to look on the bright side. Five years later, I started to think of Sam again and couldn't understand why. I had tried to start dating again but there was something bothering me and for some reason I started to look for people I had known in the past. I began searching the Internet looking for Sam. I was curious to see how her life had turned out and if we could strike up a renewed friendship, although I didn't want to interfere with her life. I just wanted to say, 'Hi, how's it going? What have you been up to for the last twenty-five years?' But as usual with my luck, I couldn't find out a thing! I spent hours looking but to no avail.

"Finally I felt so compelled to find her that I contacted a private detective; I wanted to know if he could find any information and as he was a retired police officer I thought he might have access to information that I couldn't access. I couldn't believe it though when he told me how much it would cost. Yikes!

"So being a divorced guy and having had to 'buy out' my ex-wife in order to keep the house, I thought I had better cool it and do my own investigation, so I joined a website called Classmates. I had tried before many times to find Sam's name listed on the roster of the school she went to, and somehow this time I found her name! However, her name was linked to an obituary which had been posted by her sister. My heart sank as I read it, but I thought, 'No way. It can't be her, she's way too young to die.' So I emailed her sister and she wrote me back confirming it was Sam. I was in shock! Here was a person that I had cared about deeply and she was gone. Now come the strange parts to this story.

"During this time I began hearing strange noises in my house. My front door slammed one night and I thought someone had either left or just shown up. I called to my daughter, 'Jessica is that you?' but got no response. I yelled again to Jessica but after again getting no response I went to her room and found her in bed. I went downstairs to investigate and found the front door locked (dead-locked) and all the other doors were locked as well. How did I manage to hear my front door close when it can only be locked from the inside?

"This happened on two separate occasions. Both times I went downstairs to investigate because the sound of that particular door closing is distinctive and both times I found the door locked. I had begun to think I was losing my marbles! My daughter often has friends over and I thought I heard them a few nights later when there was a stomping noise coming up the stairs and going into my daughter's bedroom; but it turned out that no-one had come over on that particular night. It was now coming up to Valentine's Day and I asked Sam's sister what they had done for her funeral; I was told that she had been cremated and her ashes had been scattered in and around a vacation beach house that the family owned. I asked her if it would be alright if I were to place some flowers where Sam's ashes were placed and her sister said that it shouldn't be a problem. I visited the beach on Valentine's Day and placed a dozen red roses in and around the point where they had scattered the ashes. I had been to that summer house with Sam twenty-five years before so going there brought deep emotions and fond memories back to me that day. I had to stay until dark to complete the flowers drop-off because I had got lost and had to ask directions from people before I could find the place again. The sound of the front door closing hasn't happened since I dropped off the roses.

"Not a day goes by that I don't think of her. Sam had divorced around the same time as me and had drunk herself to death. According to her sister, her whole world simply fell apart after her divorce and she became a recluse, never leaving her townhouse; the family tried to get help for her but she refused. She had lost her driving licence and was arrested a few times for being drunk and disorderly. Maybe what she needed was a beat-up old fireman to perform one more rescue to try and save her, and I would have tried by giving it my all because she was someone that I had loved. But unfortunately I was never given the chance."

G is for Grounding

"Putting your hands in the earth is very grounding, if you'll excuse the pun."

—JOHN GLOVER

The key to spiritual development is to learn how to 'ground', to 'anchor' or 'earth' yourself. Grounding is imperative if you are going to work with spirit, as it ensures that you remain rooted to your physical body. Even if you feel you are not ready to work with spirit yet, grounding yourself on a daily basis will help you feel centred and more focused. Try it for a week initially and feel the difference. Notice how you are not feeling so drained especially when being around someone who normally takes your energy. I make sure that I ground and put psychic light around myself twice every day, morning and night.

Grounding is about being aware that we are in a physical body but, at the same time, endeavouring to become spiritual workers and healers. Prior to opening up to the spirit world or carrying out any form of healing such as Reiki, it is imperative to ground and protect yourself so that you do not feel dizzy, disorientated, or take on the physical ailments of a client or patient. From a mediumistic point of view, it helps to protect and balance from any negative energy. So how do we ground and protect?

If you are holding on to any negative energies or worry, bring that energy down to the ground from your crown chakra, to your feet and into the ground. Once you have done this, you are ready to ground by connecting yourself to the core of the Earth. In order to do this, simply imagine growing thick and sturdy roots from the soles of your feet and linking with Mother Earth. Once you have visualised this, you are ready to put a form of protection around yourself.

Protect yourself by imagining a ball of energy over the top of your head which opens and sends a beautiful ethereal white light down through your crown chakra, past your throat chakra, heart chakra and solar plexus, down and down, through your legs and finally your feet. Then bring that white light around the outside of your body so you are totally cocooned in a protective bubble of light.

I like to 'cloak myself' over the white light so that I feel a double protection. Imagine a large cloak in purple. The cloak reaches the floor, the sleeves are very long and the cloak has a large hood. To ensure full protection, button the cloak up to the neck and put the hood up.

My friend Joey protects himself before working with spirit, with a 'psychic condom'! He says this is a fabulous form of protection. Imagine pulling a massive condom up over your body. You are completely covered and therefore protected from any negative energy.

You will know if you are ungrounded if you have:

- a feeling of being forgetful and lethargic;
- a feeling of nausea or dizziness;
- negative thoughts or actions;
- procrastination;
- a feeling of anger towards yourself or others;
- a feeling of low emotion or depression.

However, please note that some of the above may also be linked to illness so consult a doctor if you are concerned in any way at all. You will know that you are grounded when you have:

- a feeling of being balanced and grounded;
- a sense of 'knowing' and being at one with yourself and others;
- a feeling of the loving guidance of higher spiritual levels;
- an ability to move forward in your life;
- a feeling of being energised and at peace with yourself and others;
- no worry or anxiety.

Please, always ensure you remember to:

- never, ever, send bad thoughts or energy out to others, as what you send out will undoubtedly come back to you – this is karma!
- drink plenty of water and walk in natural surroundings. Hug a tree!
- do something nice and unexpected for someone;
- be purposeful in everything you do;

- visualise colour in your meditations and note the meaning of each colour, such as green for healing, red for grounding, yellow for knowledge, white for purity, etcetera.

H is for Haunted Properties

"My dear sir, it haunted me for the rest of my life."

—PETER O'TOOLE

Although most people that you would ask about this would say old properties, or buildings that house many people such as prisons, hospitals, castles, etcetera, are the most likely to be haunted, the reality is that ANY property can be haunted – even modern ones. However, the likelihood is that more old properties tend to have the 'haunted feeling' about them, as they have more history and habitation than newer buildings.

What feelings does one have in a 'haunted' property?
- being watched or 'spied on';
- someone standing close behind you;
- being touched by unseen hands;
- the hair on the back of your neck standing up;
- cobwebby fingers on your face or body;
- a cold breeze as if someone has walked past you;
- a dark, depressing feeling especially in one particular area.

What are the signs that indicate a building is haunted?
- lights turning on and off or up and down on their own;
- light bulbs blowing frequently;
- sounds of items being dropped but when you go to investigate there is nothing there;
- seeing unexplained shadows from the corner of your eye;

- strange behaviour from pets in the property, such as dogs barking or growling at something you cannot see, or cats staring in a particular area as if they can see someone;
- hearing voices of people, or whispers, or someone calling your name;
- seeing twinkling lights, mists or unexplained moving shapes;
- sudden temperature drops especially in one area of the property.

Of course these are just a few examples of what you can feel or see or sense in a haunted property.

Who is haunting the building, and why?

This is the big question, and I have been in many haunted buildings now as co-host on the Rescue Mediums show in Canada. Here are a few examples of who we come across whilst filming on the show.

- An angry man who had lost most of his family on Earth, had turned against God and was going over and over the trauma of losing his loved ones, not believing that he could go to the light because he felt he didn't deserve to.
- A soldier, who had died violently on the battlefield and kept going over and over the awful conditions he experienced during that time.
- A male spirit who had encountered an awful childhood with his bullying father. When his father came forward to greet him as we sent the younger male to the light, he refused to acknowledge his father and walked right past him into his mother's arms.
- Unknown and definitely unwelcome spirits who kept coming through a portal when a young girl 'played' with a ouija board.

H is also for Healing

"The practice of forgiveness is our most important contribution to the healing of the world."

—MARIANNE WILLIAMSON

I have been practising Reiki for twelve years and am a Reiki Master, teaching others how to become Reiki healers themselves. I also practise Angel Harmonic Healing, which involves working with the archangels in order to heal and bring back balance to the body spiritually, mentally, emotionally and physically. I have also undertaken the first and second degrees in Angelic Reiki. Healing is a way of life for me and I often pick up if there is a shift of universal energy where people (especially sensitives) are feeling out of balance and I will send healing to all who need it.

I is for Inspirational Writing

"There is no greater agony than bearing an untold story inside you."

—MAYA ANGELOU

I have shared some of my own examples of inspirational writing earlier on in the book. This isn't something I do all the time, just when I feel what I call 'the pull' which is where my hands start to 'itch' and I have to pick up a pen or pencil and start writing. The information usually flows freely as it is coming direct from spirit so I don't have to think about what I am putting. All I have to do is trust. Very often, similar to when I am doing psychic art, I don't know what I have put onto the paper until I am finished. Inspirational writing is something that you will develop through practice and belief. Why don't you try it?

K is for Karma

"How people treat you is their karma; how you react is yours."

—WAYNE DYER

This is a subject I get asked a lot about and, without getting too technical or heavy, karma means 'action' or 'to do'. It's the law of cause and effect, and the law of karma as denoted in the basic Buddhism guides states that if you send out bad thoughts or do a bad deed especially if premeditated - if it is conscious and deliberate – then, in effect, the same will come back to you. Most people have heard of the Biblical phrase, 'As ye sow, so also shall ye reap' and the quotation of Jesus Christ, "Do unto others as you would have them do unto you." A more modern expression that most of you will be familiar with is, "What goes around comes around." So if you are sending out loving thoughts and practising loving deeds then you have nothing to worry about because karma won't come and bite you on the behind!

L is for the Law of Attraction

"Minds are like flowers, they only open when the time is right."

—STEPHEN RICHARDS

There's a lot in the saying 'What you put out, you get back'. For example, when you are out and about in your car do you think, "Oh no, I am driving behind the slowest driver in the world – again!" You expected this to happen so the universe will give you what you expect. So how can you turn this around? A lot of it has to do with living in the moment and being thankful for the good things around us. How can you attract what you want for the future if your head is all over the place in the here and now?

There are so many publications and inspirational speakers who will tell you what the law of attraction is all about. However, the only person who can change your life for the better is YOU. I admit I do get a little annoyed when I hear people saying things like, "Good things never happen to me" or when they get lazy and expect others to do things for them. Even in readings, it is obvious from the messages I am receiving from spirit that the client has to do some work themselves to get out of the rut they are in, so that they can move forward in their life.

There is nothing more rewarding than doing something for yourself and feeling that sense of achievement. Firstly, you need to find your own power; it may be deep-rooted so think about how you feel right now and what you want to release from your life. Now write it down and recognise how you feel. Don't worry if you feel emotional as this is part of the releasing process – you are bidding farewell to the old and saying hello to the new.

I remember the first time I did this exercise I shocked myself into action as I didn't realise how unhappy and low I had been feeling. It was at that point when the penny finally dropped and I began to understand the power of my own mind. In life we create our own blockages by procrastinating; pay attention to your thoughts and feelings and be determined to turn your life around. Now write down what you love about yourself. You can do this! Enjoy writing down what you have achieved and are proud of in your life and notice how different you feel, seeing positive words and attributes on paper.

The Law of Attraction will bring us what we expect in life so if we expect the best, that is what we will receive. Remember to have self-respect and love the fact that you are a wonderful and unique human being. When I was growing up my uncle used to say, "There's no such word as can't" – how very wise and true those words were. Believe in yourself and feel enlightened, because anything is possible. If you are short of money and could do with a little abundance in your life, why not try the following exercise?

Manifesting money into your life

"Don't let anything stand in the way of you claiming and manifesting the life that you choose rather than the life you have by default."

—JOY PAGE

Find somewhere quiet to sit where you won't be disturbed; relax your mind and body and focus on how much money you desire. You may find that an amount just pops into your head and if this is the case, go with it. Visualise that amount in your mind's eye in the form of a cheque. See the amount made payable to you by the universe with today's date. It is official – that money belongs to you. Now visualise yourself holding the cheque in your hand and imagine a bright white light around your body as you hold the cheque. How does it feel in your hand? What shape is the cheque? Look again at the amount which is clear and concise and say the following affirmation out loud: "My life flows with abundance, and I deserve the riches of life."

Carry out this exercise for as long as it takes for you truly to believe the money will manifest. As you get more proficient, focus your intention on what you will use the money for. If it's a new car, clear out your garage to make a space for your new car; buy a new air freshener and visualise yourself sitting at the wheel of your dream car, driving along in the sunshine smelling its newness.

M is for Meditation

"Feelings come and go like clouds in a windy sky. Conscious breathing is my anchor."

—THICH NHAT HANH

Everyone is different and, as such, developing clairvoyance is a personal journey for each and every one of us. For me, meditation will always be the key to understanding my inner self. Through experience I have learned to still my mind and 'simply be'. Meditating will help you to live a happy, peaceful and spiritual life. It is the answer to many people's prayers as they go on inward journeys they could never have dreamed of in the past. It is a way of relaxing, just letting that chattering mind subside and enjoying the peace and tranquillity that only meditating can bring. Once you learn how to focus your mind and be able to go to a special place such as the countryside, a beautiful garden or anywhere else you would like to visit, it won't take long before you start to relax and enjoy meditating. Remember that you can contact your local Spiritualist Church to join in guided meditations or to join a psychic circle.

Never try to open up to the spirit world (opening the chakras) on your own without experienced tuition. Always remember to ground and put psychic white light around yourself prior to meditation. Occasionally I like to write down my meditations and find it very interesting looking back on them. Here is a selection.

Angel healing

I was in the desert on a camel with Zamil and Ruby riding alongside me. The meditation was very vivid to the point where I could feel the swaying of the camel and the warmth of its body. The sun was warm on my face and I was wearing long cotton robes in white. We came to a building, a marble domed healing temple with a silver door. Inside was a beautiful white angel and I could see cherubs everywhere. There were little silver star lights on the ceiling and a white fur rug. A huge sparkly amethyst geode twinkled in the corner and a picture that I had either designed myself or painted was hanging on the wall in a frame; there was also a fish tank with brightly coloured fish. I was asked by the white angel to lie on the therapy bed and she healed my heart and head with love, pulling my worries out on a silver thread which she then tied into a bundle and threw outside letting the soft sand and the wind carry them away.

After my meditation I was compelled to pick up my pen and start writing and I could feel slight pressure on my hand. I trusted this and wrote: "Sometimes we feel with our heart, and other times with our soul. We need that soul connection which takes us to a higher vibrational field where we can 'feel' on a different level. You will benefit from some soul-cleansing and we, your angels, will help you to do this in the right way. Be by water and imagine all your worries spilling over into the water where they will be carried away forever. Listen to your heart and deep within your soul, for good things are coming your way. Have patience, and BELIEVE. Soul stories are the thing of the future and you are to write all about them, sharing your wisdom and experiences with others. Believe..."

After this, I went into another meditation. I was flying on the back of the white horned Pegasus who took me to the Halls of Knowledge. I was greeted by a gentleman who ushered me to some water where I swam with turtles, which was a truly beautiful experience. I could see a house in the distance so I came out of the water, dried myself and walked through a field of bright blue cornflowers. My Grandma was sitting in the field. She told me that my Dad (her son) was helping and protecting me and she told me that I would be writing about my memoirs. Before she left, she gave me a coin as a gift.

A premonition

A number of years ago when I was developing my gift in Jackie's class we were being led through a meditation in the circle and for some reason I did a detour and Jackie's voice faded completely into the background. I 'found myself' walking along Guardamar beach in Spain, which is one of my favourite places, and everything was so vivid I actually felt that I was there. All the colours, sounds and smells were heightened and I could see the sand glistening as I walked up the beach. After a while I saw a man sitting cross-legged on the beach so I walked over to him. He looked up at me and said, "Hello Alison, I'm Peter." That was all he said, but I felt he was a very spiritual person and I knew I would meet him in the future. All too soon we were guided back to the present and when I described the man as well as mentioning his name to Jackie, she said, "Alison, you have met Peter, Joey's mentor who is one of the most spiritual people I have ever met."

The first time I met Peter was a year later when having coffee on the main street in Gibraltar with our friends Joey and Rose and they introduced him to me. I told him about my meditation and he wasn't surprised at all – he just asked if he was fully clothed! I confirmed that he was. We had a conversation about my forthcoming angel workshop which was to be the first one of many. I had a gap in the content and mentioned this to Peter who suggested I include 'quiet plenitude' where everyone sat in silence and inwardly thanked their angels for their blessings. I did as he suggested and it was a beautiful moment for everyone in the room as we felt the connection between us all and the peace and tranquillity surrounding us.

A couple of years later John and I were standing on the balcony of our hotel in Gibraltar admiring the view, when there in front of us was a large white feather floating down. We both saw it and there were no birds flying overhead. I knew that the angels were with us that day. Later on that afternoon we were sitting in the bar at the hotel having a coffee when a man walked past John who leaned over to me and said, "Ali, I'm sure that's Peter." I thought he had mistaken him for someone else because what would Peter be doing in our hotel? But as the man turned round, sure enough it was him. I called him over and he was so excited to see us as we hugged each other. Peter linked in with me and gave me a message from my spirit guide and I in turn gave him messages from his angels which comforted both of us. It was obvious we were destined to meet at this time in our lives.

Earlier on that day as John and I were in the town, he had said he wanted to go back to the hotel. I asked why, but he said he didn't know, he just wanted to go back and didn't want to remain in the town. The most amazing thing was that after Peter had gone, John admitted that he had been looking out for Peter in the town as he had meditated earlier on, asking his spirit guides to help find him. He wondered why he'd had a burning desire to go back to the hotel and I remember thinking it was strange at the time. Well of course his guides knew that Peter was on his way to our hotel even if we didn't!

Angel presence

During one afternoon, I was sitting in my meditation room at the top of our garden. I had done my grounding and psychic protection, and had my eyes closed. All of a sudden, the top part of the 'stable' door opened. It was as if a gust of wind had opened the door, but there didn't seem to be any wind at all. Part-way through my meditation, I heard a soft thud and a loud purring as our white fluffy cat Celestial (known as Celeste for short) jumped onto my knee. I thought this was very strange as she has never jumped over the door of the meditation room before, and I sensed that she could feel the lovely angelic vibrations in the room and was reacting to them, purring loudly as she cuddled into me on my lap.

Spirit guide shuffle!

Although I do meditate (maybe not as much as I should), it would take me years to write down every single account. However, I wanted to share this experience with you as it proves that although it's nice to prepare for meditation in the usual way with relaxing music, candles and incense burning, this is not always the way due to our busy lives. If our spirit guides need to give us information they will send us on what I call a 'mini meditation'. Here is a great example of the mini meditation.

This morning I was rushing around as usual. John had gone to the hospital for his weekly blood test and I had showered, dressed and fussed the pets who had come to greet me upstairs; I was about to run downstairs for my cup of tea before dashing out of the door. However, my spirit guides had other ideas! I was told yesterday at a Mind Body and Spirit fair that my guides were having 'a shuffle about' and although I had felt this I wasn't sure in what way - until now, that is.

I felt I had to stand still and close my eyes. As I did so, Star, one of my guides whom I hadn't encountered for some time, came forward. I know when she is around as she leaves little stars everywhere and I should have been more aware yesterday at the MBS as, when I walked in, I saw little silver and gold stars all over the floor and stars on the front cover of a book I bought. Anyway, I digress! She told me to sit down (in the mini-meditation, not physically) so I did as she asked. She told me that for now Zamil and Ruby have taken a step back as there are many changes coming in. She said my Indian chief is still around me, although I still don't know his name (so I just call him The Wise One – it's certainly befitting and it will have to do for now!). Star handed me a large yellow feather and said that whenever I feel drained or I am not sure what to do, I must imagine holding the yellow feather and all will become clear. She said it was important that I finished my book and that my guides will help me to focus so that the words will flow.

She also told me that the tortoise was my power animal at present and to look up the meaning. I had to laugh when I read that the tortoise is asking me to have patience, that everything will be apparent in good time!

What she said next though is the main reason I had to write this down straight away. I was asked to wrap healing around each page of my book in its rough and original state. *This healing will transfer through each stage of the printing process and each person who buys the book and starts to read it will feel healing energy through their hands.* I didn't question this because it made so much sense. As a Reiki Master and Angel Healer, I promote loving intent and spreading the light to others. I often send distant healing to the past, present and future, to people, animals, and plants. Why not be able to send healing to each and every person who will pick up my book so that as they turn each page, they will feel the love, light and healing of their spirit guides and the angels?

N is for Nature

"Man's heart away from nature becomes hard."

—STANDING BEAR

I love Mother Nature in all her glory and I enjoy the seasons we have in the UK. Springtime is my favourite season as it is all about new life and growth and brings with it new hope and lighter nights. I live in a rural part of Cheshire and I remember last year going on a trip to London with a good friend. It was exciting and I enjoyed going for a trip to the theatre, a shopping trip and the experience of riding on the Tube. However I felt really tired and 'out of sorts'. When I came home I took the dogs out for a walk and as I was walking in our beautiful countryside I stopped in my tracks and let out a contented sigh. I was home! There were no crowds, no noise and no pollution. Just me and Mother Nature – it was bliss.

N is also for 'No Ordinary Moments'

"With the past I have nothing to do; nor with the future. I live now."

—RALPH WALDO EMERSON

Have you ever wondered why the best things in life are presented to us when we are simply 'being' and enjoying ourselves? That is because we are totally relaxed and in a positive state of mind. Problems occur when we are 'living in the past' or looking too far ahead into the future. Once you bring your consciousness back to the present and listen to your inner voice you will start living life to the full.

The principle sounds easy and I admit it's harder to put into practice, but with a positive frame of mind and determination you could change your life forever. The key is to know what you want which is not as easy as it sounds! Most people when asked this question don't really know what they want: however most know what they *don't* want. Because we are then creating negative thoughts, the universe will assume that this is what we want and will grant us exactly what we have asked for albeit unconsciously. If we carry on this way, we miss the wonderful and synchronistic events that occur every minute of every day.

One of the best films I have seen that puts all of this into perspective is The Peaceful Warrior. It's about letting go of the ego and living in the moment. If you do just that, you will live life to the full and appreciate the journey. There is a part in the film where the main character is in his usual state of polishing his ego when suddenly everything slips into slow motion. For once, he has a peripheral view of everything that is going on around him at that moment and the way it's portrayed is truly beautiful. It's a classic example of what you could miss if you are not paying attention, and there is a line in the film that says it all: "There are no ordinary moments."

O is for Ouji Boards

"Nothing is more terrible than to see ignorance in action."

—JOHANN WOLFGANG VON GOETHE

A ouija board is a dangerous 'game' which can be bought freely in certain countries. When working on Rescue Mediums in Canada, one of our homeowners shared a story with us about hunting for a gift at Christmas for a young female relative only to come across a pink ouija board for girls in their local toyshop!

Both Jackie and I were aghast at this as it was quite obvious that people don't know how dangerous the board can be. An awful lot of the psychic investigations we deal with are caused by people not knowing how to use a ouija board properly, and the misuse of this 'game' causes dark and sometimes dangerous entities to come through a portal in the property which remains open, inviting other spirits to come through. If this has happened to you, you will need to call in an experienced medium to close the portal for you.

I would not recommend the ouija to anyone – far from being fun, they can be downright dangerous. On one of our shows, two lovely young sisters had 'played' with the ouija board in their own home and in the home of their friend. What happened was they were keeping a portal door wide open as an invitation for spirits of a lower plane to come through. So much so, that one of the entities took over the personality of one of the girls to the point where she felt possessed. When she looked in the mirror she saw another girl's face instead of her own; her family also said she would go off to the woods on her own where they would often find her sitting down by a stream gazing into space.

Her mother was beside herself with worry when she rang our producer to plead for the rescue mediums to investigate the spooky goings on. During the Show and Tell, Jackie and I had to stress to the family never, ever to use the ouija board again. This family had found out first-hand how this 'game' can wreak havoc on a close-knit family and cause a usually peaceful home to be full of negative energies. Needless to say the girls have said they will never use the ouija again.

O is also for Orbs

"Foolery, sir, does walk about the Orb like the sun; it shineth everywhere."

—WILLIAM SHAKESPEARE

Orbs are a fascinating phenomenon and something I have been interested in for years. But what defines an orb? Orbs are a solid or transparent 'ball' of energy or light caught on video, film, or more recently by digital cameras. Orbs are easy to see when photographs are developed and have been scientifically proven often to be caused by dust particles or malfunctioning camera diodes. However, orbs are believed by many people to be life-forms of those that once inhabited a physical body here on Earth. Ghostly orbs are the most photographed anomalies caught on film, especially by ghost hunters. They can be completely transparent or display themselves in colour. I have taken photographs before in which the orb on film appears to show a face.

It is said that a culmination of orbs that appear on photographs taken outside on a wet night are most certainly going to be caused by moisture in the air from rain drops. But what about the orbs that appear over the same people's heads at differing times of their life, and in different venues? It also leaves a question mark over why orbs often appear in photographs of mediums when they are 'open' to the spirit world and are also around the hands of healers when they are carrying out Reiki treatments or Angel Healing.

An example of recurring orbs around the same person is when I take photographs of one of my small granddaughters. As soon as she could sit up and we started taking photographs of her propped up in bed, for example, there was always an orb over her head. A couple of years ago John and I took her to the police children's Christmas party. There were lots of children there having fun and running around. When Father Christmas came in they waited patiently for him to call their name. When he called Olivia's name, she went up to him to collect her present so I saw an opportunity and took a photograph of her. Although there were lots of other children around her, there it was again, just the one orb over her head. Is this someone protecting her? I would certainly like to think so. There are other theories concerning orbs. On looking through differing sites whilst doing my research, some people believe that orbs could be nature spirits or airborne protoplasm which you would find under a microscope, only far, far more advanced. On Rescue Mediums, lots of photographs have been taken of us 'in action' and also relaxing. It's interesting that most of the 'orb' photographs appear in what is deemed to be the most haunted room in the homeowners' house.

O is also for One-Ness

"Each time a man looks into your eyes, he is only searching to find himself; for he knows already that he is part of you."

—JEREMY ALDANA

One-ness is the concept that we are all unique individuals having our own experiences in life and yet at the same time being aware of universal energy and the fact that we are all connected. I wrote a poem recently (below) which is my way of explaining the bigger picture of life itself and enjoying oneself in the process. To me it gives the true meaning of one-ness - belief.

All you have to do is believe, by reaching out to the stars and catching the brightest one. Make a wish and know deep within your heart that your dreams will come true. Be aware of universal energy around every living thing and rejoice. Let your hair down, sing, dance and walk amongst the trees taking in the sights, sounds and colours of Mother Nature. Be kind to animals and those less fortunate than yourself. Do a good deed for another and you will reap rewards you would never have imagined. Never let anyone take your energy or tell you what to do. Stand your ground and embrace the fact that you are unique – there is only one of you, and you have made your mark here on Earth. It is fabulous to be different – how boring it would be if we were all the same. Make decisions from the depths of your heart and know that you are a beautiful child of the universe. Clear your mind through meditation and deep soul-cleansing so you can feel positive movement forward. Communicate with the angels who will carry your worries and fears away forever. Everything is achievable, everything is possible and the answer to everything is love. Love yourself and watch your spirit soar as free as a bird. Give thanks for all the wonderful things around you. Embrace your life – it is not a test, it is not a play – life is real, so know that life is for living and you can do whatever you want to do. Remember – all you have to do is believe.

P is for Past Lives

"The love that you withhold is the pain that you carry lifetime after lifetime."

—ALEX COLLIER

There is a past life when a soul is reborn into a different body and era. I find past lives intriguing and I can usually tell when I meet someone if they are 'an old soul'. I can't explain this feeling other than it is a 'knowing' – a glow around their aura, or something in their eyes that denotes they have definitely been here before. Some believe that we can be reincarnated if we still have lessons to learn from our previous life.

Although people don't actively remember their previous life there is often something that triggers this, such as a déjà vu feeling when you enter a building that you have never been in before, or hearing a particular song that seems to take you back to a completely different era that seems uncannily familiar.

There are many books that have been written on the subject and some believe that it links strongly with karma. For example, your personality traits in this life can be triggered by those in a past life, whether you were generous, kind-hearted or a bad person. Some also believe that your talents in this life are likely to have been caused by past lives. Karmic consequences are what make you the person you are if you still have lessons to learn – for example, you should be more generous, stand your own ground, etcetera.

Patterns and occurrences that happen in your life time and time again could be a sign that you need to deal with the situation and move on, which means you have dealt with at least one of your karmic consequences from a previous life which will be erased from your blueprint. The choice is yours.

You can call upon the elemental angels of air to help give you peace and strength if you need assistance with a previous incarnation or past life regression. The element of air is connected to the soul and powers of the mind. Therefore, the angels of air will assist in dispelling any negativity from past lives to help to bring new and positive ideas to fruition so you will be able to recognise fresh opportunities and ventures coming your way.

P is also for Pets

"Our perfect companions never have fewer than four feet."

—COLETTE

It's a well known fact that stroking a pet can bring down your heart rate, not to mention your stress levels. I love animals and there is a lovely flow of 'chi' through my house which I feel is partly attributed to my pets Libby the Labrador and my two cats, Celeste and Tara. Libby is gentle and loving and she absolutely adores our grandchildren. I would describe her as not having a bad bone in her body and if there was ever a gentle and happy soul, she is it. My cat Celeste is a big white furry girl with a black tail and she is drawn to my meditation room especially when I am doing readings for clients. I know that she is picking up on the loving energies of my guides and angels but I can't let her into the room when I am working! Tara is a tortoiseshell with lovely markings. She looks really sweet but is a true hunter and I have come downstairs many mornings to find a decapitated mouse at the bottom of the stairs.

I feel that having at least one pet in the house makes it a happy home and our pets don't answer us back. All they ask in return for their unconditional love is to be petted, walked (if relevant), some food to eat and somewhere warm and cosy to sleep. Not much to ask, is it? Some owners really do know how much joy their pet has brought them and will do anything to help even when the pet is in old age. I have never read anything so heart-warming as a story which was on AOL news one August. It was a piece from the Pioneer Press and there was a beautiful snap of an owner lovingly cradling his arthritic dog who was nineteen years of age, in the warm waters of Lake Superior, in order to lull him to sleep. The story certainly melted my heart...

One of the hardest things ever is when we lose our pets to the spirit world. I have lost two of my furry friends which I was devastated about but I know their souls live on. I hope this helps if you have also lost a pet to spirit.

Love transcends all boundaries and I am often asked if I can communicate with pet spirits. Although it is obvious that a pet can't 'talk' to me, I can pass on information to clients when they come to see me for a reading. I will often see their loved one in spirit holding a cat, rabbit or bird or with a dog lying by their feet. I feel blessed to be able to pass on such wonderful confirmation to people that our pets' souls live on. No-one will ever know for sure where our pets go when they pass on. Some say they go to 'the rainbow bridge' where they can run and play amongst the trees and beautiful rolling hills. Others feel that the pet goes to the same place as our human loved ones. I am sure that some of you will have already felt your pet's spirit around you in the home, which is further information that they are absolutely fine and are just popping by to say "Hello".

P is also for Portal

Many people ask me what a portal is and I have encountered several since working on the show. Basically, a portal or gate is an energy field through which unwanted forces can come through. They are usually created by someone summoning demons, working with the dark arts or misusing a ouija board. Once opened, a portal is a doorway for spirit to pass through, often causing havoc in the home as there is no control over which type of spirit come through. Many are of a very low vibration and as the portal remains open they will continue to come through until the door is closed and sealed by someone with relevant experience. If you stand by a portal you can feel dizzy, off-balance and cold and when I stood in front of one on the show, I felt as if a dark force was trying to suck me inside so I moved very quickly!

The safest way to avoid opening a portal in your home is never to dabble in the 'dark arts' and never to play with a ouija board. If you feel that you have a portal in your home, contact a reputable medium with rescue work experience who will confirm the situation either way. If they state that there is a portal, they will be able to communicate with the spirits, sending them on their way, and they will close and seal the portal.

There may be residual energy after such a strong force in the home so smudging a room, using crystals or praying or using positive mantras will help. After Jackie and I had closed a portal in one of the homes on the show I 'drew' the Reiki symbols over the walls and doors of the property, particularly in the room where the portal had been opened, to promote healing energies back into the room and to cleanse the area. Never try to attempt to open or close a portal yourself – it can be very dangerous.

P is also for Psychometry

"Here we are, trapped in the amber of the moment. There is no why."

—KURT VONNEGUT

Universal energy is around every living thing and this concept has been brought to life by the insights of James Redfield in his book The Celestine Prophecy. But is there a link between energy and inanimate objects? Have you ever picked something up belonging to someone else and had an instant feeling such as unexplained emotions or seeing an image in your mind's eye that seems to appear from nowhere? If this has happened to you, then you have without knowing it experienced psychometry, which is the ability to understand the history of an object through the sense of touch.

The term psychometry was coined by the American physician and Professor of Physiology, Joseph Rhodes Buchanan, in 1842 from the Greek words psyche, which means 'soul', and metron, meaning 'measure'. Buchanan worked with his students by placing various drugs in glass vials and asking them to identify the drugs by holding the vials. He was amazed at their accuracy which was highlighted in his book Journal of Man. He suggested that all objects have 'souls' that retain memory. It is my belief that everyone is born with a psychic gift, also known as one's 'sixth sense' or 'knowing'. You only have to watch a child playing with their 'imaginary friend' or listen to the wise words that emanate from a toddler's lips and you are left wondering, "Where on Earth did that come from?" Well, the answer lies within – they are using their natural psychic gift which sadly, if it isn't nurtured as they get older, will fade in the mists of time. They learn new things and either forget their inner psychic or they are discouraged from developing it by their parents or teachers.

Another way of explaining the feeling you get from your inner psyche is when you sense that something is wrong, or you get a negative feeling about someone that is uncannily accurate. This is known as your intuition, or 'gut feeling'. Unfortunately, in our busy materialistic world not everyone recognises when they've experienced a natural psychic moment.

I use the divination tool of psychometry in order to make a connection with my clients. I usually hold a personal object belonging to the person such as a piece of jewellery, keys, a mobile 'phone or a glove. The object retains that person's energy or spiritual impressions and, by linking in, I will receive messages which can be similar to a camera film or tape recorder. For example, if the object has been passed down through the family, such as an heirloom, the information will also include the history of its previous owners.

You can have fun with the following exercise and you may surprise yourself into the bargain! Ask a few of your friends round to your house and tell them to bring a personal item with them such as a piece of jewellery or any metallic item, which is an excellent conductor of energy. Place your individual objects into a basket. No peeking! You won't get the benefit of this if you see who has put which object into the basket.

Indicate an agreed time in which to perform the exercise – say fifteen minutes to start with, and remove an item (not your own) and find somewhere quiet to sit. Ensure you feel relaxed, then place the item in one hand and place your other hand over the top. As you start to tune in and images, words or impressions pop into your mind, jot these down on a piece of paper. Remember that the majority of information you receive won't make any sense to you as it is for someone else, so when you are relaying your information ensure you give the person everything you have received and don't try to analyse anything. Share the information you have received in exactly the way it was 'given' to you. If you don't feel you have got much the first time you try psychometry, don't be too hard on yourself. Like everything, it all boils down to practise.

Q is for Quiet Plenitude

"Reverie is not a mind vacuum. It is rather the gift of an hour which knows the plenitude of the soul."

—GASTON BACHELARD

Sometimes it's just nice to find a quiet place, put on some gentle music, burn some incense or aromatherapy oil and relax. We don't always have to meditate and hope a message comes through – one of the loveliest things we can do is just 'simply be'. I share this exercise with everyone at my Angel Breath workshops and it's a beautiful exercise to carry out whether alone or in a group.

R is for Rescue Work And Rescue Mediums!

"Come out, come out, wherever you are."

—THE FILM THE SHINING (1980)

Earlier on in the book I have shared with you some of the scariest shows on Rescue Mediums as well as giving you a first-hand account of what I experience when we are filming for the show from emails I send to my husband in England. What I love about rescue work is the fact that as rescue mediums we don't just go into a place and say, "Yes, it's haunted!" What we do is try to help the spirit who is causing the activity. They are stuck in this world for whatever reason and we will do whatever we can to send them to where they need to go to rest. Who knows sometimes why spirits don't go to the light? It is our job to try and find out and we never, ever judge. Here is a reply I sent to a fan of Rescue Mediums when she asked how long a spirit can be Earthbound for. I hope this goes some way to explain the complexities of the work we do.

"This is a condensed version of the subject! There is no time in the spirit world, so what we would deem as 'eternity' would not be the same, therefore it would be very difficult to put a time-frame on how long the spirit has been Earthbound. It could actually feel a short time to them when in fact it could have been a very long time in our sense of the word.

What gives Jackie and me clues about time-frames is when we 'see' the spirit and can describe what we see around them, such as property, mode of transport, their clothing, etcetera.

"I believe that when spirits are afraid to pass over to the spirit world for whatever reason such as fear, confusion or misunderstanding, they stay until they get someone's attention by whatever means possible - by making noises, creating cold spots, moving objects (to name but a few). This will then often carry on and get stronger as the spirit tries desperately to attract someone's attention because of their plight and wanting to tell their story. They will very often go over the same scenario or incident within their life so it seems like a stuck record or the same video playing over and over again.

"It is not a good idea to have a spirit hanging around a property for a long time because as Jackie and I have found on the show, the longer they are 'stuck' here on Earth, the more they will drain the people living in the house making them feel lethargic or unwell. This can also drastically affect the energies in the property as well. Once such a problem has been identified, the best thing to do is to try to communicate with that spirit, find out as much about who they were on Earth, and guide them over to the light so they are not hanging around for a long time.

"A spirit may stay Earthbound because they feel they have some unfinished business to deal with here on Earth before they will go to the light. One of the best portrayals of this is in the film Ghost."

A Rescue Mediums ditty!

This is doing the rounds on Facebook at present and, although I take the work I do very seriously, there has to be an element of fun in what we do otherwise what would be the point of anything? So here is a little poem I wrote – not the best in the world I know, but people loved it because it gave them a giggle.

The Rescue Mediums ladies send spirits to the light;
by gathering clues from psychic art they sometimes get a fright!
But on they go to help the folk who live in the haunted house
and use their psychic antennae and are as quiet as a mouse!
It's hard work for the ladies when the spirit won't communicate,

but they persevere and slog right on all the way through the night.
On they go regardless and with the help of their trusted guide
they send the wayward spirit to their loved ones on the other side.

S is for Shamanism

> *"Being satisfied with what we already have is a magical golden key to*
> *being alive in a full, unrestricted and inspired way."*
>
> —PEMA CHODRON

The practice of shamanism has been around for thousands of years. Shamans can travel to a different layer within the universe by going into an altered state of consciousness. One of the basic principles of shamanism is that everything has a spirit and is alive, and shamans often go into a trance by dancing, meditating and drumming with drums decorated with bells, rattles or bones, which denote different spirits and animals. Shamans are natural healers and can treat sickness and illness. They work closely with animal spirit guides also known as 'power' or 'totem' animals which act as message-bearers or omens, as well as looking into the spiritual meaning of that particular animal.

S is also for Spirit Guides

> *"The only question is: does this path have a heart? If it does, then it is a*
> *good path; if it doesn't, then it is of no use."*
>
> —CARLOS CASTENEDA

Everyone has a spirit guide – but who are they? Well, one of the questions I get asked a lot is, "What's the difference between a spirit guide and a guardian angel?" The only way I can describe the difference is that our guardian angels are purely 'angels' and they have never inhabited a human body. Within the book Spiritual Unfoldment by White Eagle, he calls the guardian angel a 'custodian of the Karmic law' which rules all life. They record all our deeds and help us to work out our own karma.

Our spirit guides are different to the angels as they have lived in a human body. They are ascended spirit from the human line of evolution and have had spiritual experiences themselves similar to those that we encounter in our own lifetime. Our spirit guides are there to help and guide us on our spiritual paths, and who best to guide us than someone who understands what it is like to have lived on Earth? Our spirit guides are now pure spirit and have no ego. Our main guide is known as our 'doorkeeper' or 'gatekeeper', and they are the one who is assigned to us before we are born to help guide us in understanding life's many lessons. These lessons could be experiences that have not been resolved from a previous life, so we have been given the chance to be reborn and find a solution to those problems in this lifetime. Your main spirit guide will stay with you throughout your entire life and helps you to fulfil your Earth mission.

Other guides may make themselves known to you at different intervals on your life's path. How you meet your spirit guide is a personal experience and is unique to you, be it through meditation or another form of spiritual development. I met my main spirit guide Zamil in a vivid dream; when I woke up, I felt loved and comforted in a way I couldn't explain. I knew without a doubt that I had met my spirit guide and a few months later I had confirmation of this whilst sitting in the garden where, when I asked, he gave me his name and also told me where he had lived when he had inhabited his human body on Earth. I have since met my other spirit guides: Ruby is my psychic art guide and has a wonderful sense of humour; Star brings with her a nature spirit quality and is often accompanied by woodland animals; Amy is a little girl spirit who works with me when I am working with spirit children.

I speak to my spirit guides every day either through meditation or a thought process, called telepathy. Our spirit guides don't have a voice box so the voice we 'hear' will sound like our own, although the messages are coming direct from the spirit world. It is much the same when I am doing clairvoyant readings for a client. I know that any messages I receive either in word form or pictorial form are given to me by spirit and I love the confirmation I receive from a client about personal messages given direct from spirit, no matter how bizarre the message appears to me! Our spirit guides never let us down.

People will meet their spirit guides through different forms of communication such as meditation or in a group situation such as a psychic circle or through their local Spiritualist Church. Whichever way you choose to develop your spirituality, please don't give up if you don't see your spirit guide at first. Your guide will develop you at a pace he or she feels is right for you and it is something that cannot be rushed. Everyone develops at a different pace and never compare yourself to others. I remember when I was in my psychic development class, I couldn't understand why others said they could see their spirit guide and all I could see of mine were long sleeves. However, looking back now, all the signs were there – I *knew* it was my guide even though I couldn't see all of him. Yes, I felt my guide was male! I could actually feel him beside me even though I couldn't 'see' all of him in my meditation. Of course, he appeared to me (all of him) in my dreams, and after that he appeared in meditations whether I was alone or part of a group and I have seen him many times since.

Never be disheartened and never feel that you have disappointed your guide as they are here to help us to learn from any mistakes we make in life. After all, we are human and our spirit guides will always be by our side in love and forgiveness. As the saying goes, 'To err is human'. Our guide's love for us is unconditional and to meet and communicate with them is a very special and humbling experience. When we take a wrong turn in life, our guides will sometimes intervene to ensure we are guided back on the right path. If you are really stuck and need an answer, ask your guide to assist you and he or she will give you a way of resolving the problem. You may have to do some 'digging' yourself to find a solution, but if you want confirmation that you are on the right path ask for a specific sign. These signs are often in the form of coincidences or synchronistic events that your spirit guide has put on your path to make you sit up and take notice! Look out for the clues – they are out there. Once you have recognised them for what they are, remember to acknowledge this by thanking your guide. After all, they really are your best friend.

To follow are a few true life stories of messages from spirit guides. These are combined from people who are just developing their psychic gift and others who know their guide is with them and have had some form of communication or evidence of such, usually when they are not even trying!

Gloria

"Two weeks ago I did a reading using my grandmother's cards for a close friend; they read an accident, warning, trouble, nurse, dark-haired older woman, legal papers, money, younger fair woman and a gift. There was another card in there, however I cannot remember what it was. Last Monday, the friend had an accident at work involving an electric hand saw and nearly amputated his hand. He is marrying a beautiful young blonde woman in August, who went to meet him at the site where he was injured and took him to the hospital. At the hospital they were attended to by a dark-haired nurse. He received the paperwork yesterday to complete for compensation. This is one of the more accurate and complete readings I have done for quite some time! And I believe I have my spirit guide to thank."

Alan

"Hi Alison. When I was about eight years old (a long time ago) I had been very ill for six weeks and the doctor was apparently very worried. I was in my parents' bed when a knock came at the bedroom door. I said "Hello" and the door opened and a grey mist, the shape of a person, came in and went to the end of the bed. I looked at it for a moment then lost my nerve and screamed for help; at the same time I was compelled to look at the picture of my Uncle Bill who was killed in WW2, which was on the mantelpiece. By the following day I started to get better; it took another month or so and the doctor was mystified, so I am told."

S is also for Spirituality

> *"Spirituality is a domain of awareness."*
>
> —DEEPAK CHOPRA

The best way that I can define spirituality is universal love. It is about the connection we have with each other which extends beyond our own world; more importantly, it's about understanding our own spiritual nature by looking within. That's where you will find all the answers! This inner knowledge is called many things such as 'your inner child', 'your true self' or 'your higher self'. It's about getting in touch with your soul and it's something that I call 'Soul Magic'.

> *"I was once afraid of people saying, 'Who does she think she is?' Now I have the courage to stand up and say 'This is who I am'."*

> —OPRAH WINFREY

I teach Soul Magic to others and I am so proud of my class now that they have developed and have the confidence to step onto their own spiritual paths. In a nutshell, Soul Magic is a magical moment where a person or event touches your soul in a way that you have never experienced before. It could be something as simple as an act of kindness out of the blue, or a compliment that makes you feel on top of the world. It's also about living in the moment and not holding on to the past or worrying about the future, and a deep inner knowledge that we are all here for a reason and to help others as well as ourselves. During my classes we start by blessing the room, and then go into a meditation to help everyone to relax – we do spiritual exercises such as an open circle, using pendulums and being able to feel our guardian angels and spirit guides around us. I use a different theme each week. For example, we could have 'power animals' one week, and Wicca the next. We have 'talk-time' where each person says what has touched their soul that week, and how their day has gone.

I have heard people say that it's as if they have woken up from a deep slumber to find that they can do whatever they want to do. It is their life and isn't life short enough not to live your dream? You are in control of your own life, you are in control of your thoughts, and never, ever let anyone else control you. You are a special and wonderful child of the universe – all you need to do is to recognise your soul's desire and you will open up to a whole new spiritual way of being.

Once you recognise that all the answers are within, you will start to move forward on your journey of self-discovery. Soul Magic can help to heighten your awareness as you dig deep down, plant your own seeds of light and watch as your soul flourishes and grows strong. As you start to develop, your vibrations will reach a higher level of spiritual consciousness. 'Magic' is believing in yourself – if you can do that, you can make anything happen.

S is also for Synchronicity

I would like to share with you a few true accounts of synchronicity at its best. I hope you enjoy them as much as I have.

A good friend

My friend experienced synchronicity first hand and here is her story in her own words.

"It was around my birthday and I was thinking about my Mum and Dad (both passed) one night in bed and wondered what had happened to their clothes and furniture after they had died. I remember saying to friends at the time to help themselves to anything from their house as I had nowhere to store anything at my own house. My husband had mentioned a few days before that when his mother died her sideboard, or bureau, which was an expensive piece of furniture, was chopped up by his brother-in-law as no-one wanted it. This may have caused me to think about my mother's and father's belongings. It was mainly the large bureau which had stuck in my mind and where it had gone.

"To set the scene, my father died in 1991 and my mother in 1992. I kept the house for twelve months and cleared it later as I was too upset to move anything at the time of their passing. My previous husband had worked voluntarily during a weekend for a number of years feeding and exercising greyhounds in Little Leigh. We had become great friends with the trainer Peter and his wife. When the trainer retired, they moved house to Littleton near Chester in 1997 and their daughter went with them. She had never married like her other two sisters even though she was a very pretty and lovely girl four years younger than me. I was upset that they were moving out of the area and we eventually lost contact. I often thought about them, and over the years when I went on trips out to Chester or North Wales I tried to look for their house, to no avail. The only detail I knew at that time was that it was located on the main Chester Road. I had their address in an old address book which I eventually found in March 2012 and kept it in my mind so I knew which house I was looking for.

"On 1st April, 2012 (two weeks after my birthday when I was thinking about Mum and Dad), my husband and I were driving home from Wales and as usual I was looking for the house. All of a sudden I shouted out, 'Stop the car, there's Peter!' After all these years of looking and never seeing him, there he was, sitting outside his house! As he saw me walking up the drive, he said, 'I know who this is!' and gave me a big hug. He said he was now 81 years of age and unfortunately his lovely wife had passed away in 2004 and I was shocked and saddened by this. She was younger than Peter and always seemed so full of life. He then told me that his daughter was inside but warned me that she may not recognise me as she had had a brain haemorrhage at the age of fifty and had just come out of hospital after being in there for eleven months. Peter said she was now fifty-one and when she came out of the house I was amazed as she recognised me straight away. She was very delicate and had also got rheumatoid arthritis so was struggling to walk. She gave me a big hug and I was saddened by how she was, after seeing her so active when we were younger. Up to now she'd had eleven operations on her head. She told me that she had forgotten her mother had died seven years before and her sister had to sit and explain this to her.

"Peter took my husband and I inside the house and said, 'Well, do you remember that?' as he pointed to a piece of furniture. I was stunned – it was my mother's and father's bureau which I had been thinking about two weeks ago! My mother's pottery shire horse was also in the house. Peter then said, 'Do you remember that?' as he pointed to my mother's favourite Lady Love kitchen unit which she had kept in the conservatory.

"After chatting he said, 'Do you remember this Harris tweed jacket?' which he was wearing, and I realised it was my Dad's best jacket. It was well worn now with some holes inside. Peter had worn it every day for the past twenty years! He then said, 'Hold on a minute' and came out with my Dad's very best overcoat. It was still in pristine condition and I felt I could still smell my Dad on it although it was obvious it wasn't a physical smell.

"My husband and I stayed chatting to Peter and his daughter for a while and Peter said they had had the house on the market for two years with plenty of visitors but no buyers. I felt it was strange because it was a beautiful house – huge, with a massive and well-kept garden. He said the house was too large for the two of them and they wanted something smaller.

"What I want to know is: was this just a coincidence or did something draw me there...? Why was Peter sitting outside the front of his house that day as I passed by in the car at exactly the same time? We were travelling slower than normal due to road works, which may be why I saw him; if we had been travelling at our normal speed it would have been impossible to make out any detail let alone recognise someone from such a distance.

"My feelings and emotions at the house felt very strong. Our little dog was with us that day and Peter and his daughter loved her and made a great fuss of her. We swapped addresses and `phone numbers and they said they would let us know if and when they moved and would give us their new details. I still can't believe it and would love to have your views on it."

My subsequent reply

"Thank you so much for this true story - I love it. This is the true meaning of divine timing and synchronicity. It is the angels' way of letting you know how much your Mum and Dad still love you, and that some of their belongings have been in a loving home with trustworthy people who have always looked after their personal items. You were meant to drive past that day at the same time Peter was outside the house, as I believe that you have given him and his family great comfort. I also believe his wife had something to do with that 'perfect timing' as well, and that she has met your Mum and Dad in the afterlife. Now that Peter has met you, I feel you will bring them some much needed luck and it won't be long until their house is sold. It's as if they were meant to see you before they sold it and moved away again. If they had, then you may never have seen them and would always wonder what happened to your Mum's and Dad's sideboard as well as their other belongings.

"Our loved ones in spirit, our guardian angels and spirit guides, often give us loving messages and signs from spirit to make us sit up and take notice so we know without a doubt that there is a dimension other than ours, and you couldn't have had a more definitive and succinct message from your Mum and Dad that their love for you is still alive. Wow."

Marcia and Molly

My friend and neighbour Marcia shared a sad but beautiful story with me. A few months ago she had to have her beloved dog Molly put down – Molly was fifteen years old. When Marcia rang her friend to share the sad news with her, the friend told her to have a drink of vodka. After putting the `phone down, she realised she didn't have any in the house so she ordered a litre bottle with her usual shopping from the Tesco delivery service. She commented to her husband that she wished she had ordered a litre and a half and not just a litre.

When Tesco delivered her shopping the driver apologised and said they didn't have any litre bottles of vodka left, but "We have brought you a litre and a half bottle instead at the same price"! Later on that evening with a glass of vodka and tonic in her hand, Marcia inwardly asked Molly if she was okay. As she switched on the radio, her favourite song was playing... When Marcia shared these 'coincidences' with me, I said that Molly was letting her know that she is fine, without a doubt. How wonderful that her lovely pet, that had been part of the family for so long, wanted Marcia not to worry and that she had reached 'the rainbow bridge' and was absolutely fine.

Sam and Michelle

"Hi Alison! Here is a great one for you. Michelle and I have been talking about getting a rescue Beagle. We have been saying that when we find our dog we will know... Well, on Tuesday we were at one of my Buddhist chanting sessions downtown and we came outside smack into a woman walking a beautiful little Beagle who jumped on Michelle and started licking her. We talked to the woman walking her and found out that 'Lea is a rescue Beagle looking for a home!' I guess we found our Beagle!"

Lisa

"I have been adding dandelion leaves to my green salads and, when I went for massage therapy, I told the therapist who said he knew that someone was going to talk about salads this morning. We then shared some wonderful conversations on how minds are opening."

Brenda

"Back in the `90s everyone was reading The Celestine Prophecy. I borrowed a copy from a young lady whom I went to for Reiki. After I read it I told my sister that she should read it. You couldn't find the book anywhere, it was sold out at bookstores and the libraries never had it in. One day my sister was driving down the road and saw something in the middle of it. She stopped to see what it was. It was a hard copy of the book! Right there in the middle of the road. She read it, loved it and gave it to me. I treasure the book `til this day. I thought it was a crazy coincidence!"

T is for Trance Mediumship

"I stand back detached and I can hear the spirit person I am channelling, but I can't hear it clearly – and then suddenly it goes blank, that's really when they are in."

—DEREK ACORAH

A trance medium is someone who is highly trained and usually with years of experience behind them. They work on a high level of vibrational consciousness and can channel spirit – sometimes appearing as though they are in a trance. The spirit will 'talk' through the consciousness of the medium, often causing their speech pattern to change. Trance mediumship was very popular in the 1860s and 1870s. When in a typical deep trance, the medium may not recall all or any of the messages conveyed while in that altered state so they are often accompanied by an assistant who will write down everything they say. To anyone watching this type of mediumship it can often be very frightening so not for the faint-hearted!

U is for Unicorns

"The unicorn – the beautiful white horse with the magical horn that heals."

—ANONYMOUS

I have loved unicorns ever since I was a little girl and I am never surprised when a unicorn appears in my meditations as they are always beautiful, peaceful and insightful. Sometimes they have wings like Pegasus, but they still always show themselves with the horn. I call this creature a 'Unipeg' and I tell my little granddaughter many bedtime stories about the Unipeg and his friends. Just like me, she loves everything about unicorns and has a favourite unicorn toy that she takes to bed with her.

Unicorns bring magic into our lives and help to bring the playfulness of our inner child to the fore. I have felt their magical essence around me on many occasions, which makes sense as I move through a shift in spiritual consciousness. Many sensitive souls have felt or seen the unicorn in meditation, more now than ever as the Earth rises through many vibrational changes. The unicorn will choose whom they appear to, as you must hold pure love in your heart. By this I mean love for yourself as well as for others. If you are feeling unbalanced they will work with pure Earth energy to help to bring you into alignment by removing negativity within your aura. You will feel immense love in your heart when touched by the essence of a unicorn. If a unicorn is your spirit animal, you have an innocence and purity about you, retaining a childlike sense of wonder and awe. You may even work with children, particularly any highly sensitive children who have psychic or intuitive gifts. You will care deeply about Mother Nature and her wonders and love working with or reading about the fairy realms and the nature spirits.

V is for Vision Board

"The painter has the universe in his mind and hands."

—LEONARDO DA VINCI

A vision board is a fabulous way of seeing your desires in life at a glance. Place it in a prominent place in the house where you can see it regularly and make sure it is at eye level and not obstructed by anything else. Write your name at the top of the board and an affirmation such as, 'I am manifesting my dreams here and now.' Place a photograph of yourself in the middle of the board and write words that denote positivity. Mine include the words 'Believe', 'Reach for the stars' and 'Universal love'. Place whatever you want to attract in your life onto your board and remember to include the things you feel grateful for in your life. For example, my vision board is a combination of spiritual things such as angels for unconditional love, flowers and trees for new growth, birds for freedom and butterflies for transformation. I have included a picture of a beautiful house in the countryside which will be my healing temple where people can come and relax, enjoy the company of like-minded people and find their true purpose in life. Be creative, include whatever you want on your vision board and believe that you will attract everything you desire. Remember to value yourself and manifest reality into your life. See yourself doing well and you will.

W is for Wichcraft (Wicca)

"The first time I called myself a witch was the most magical moment of my life."

—MARGOT ADLER

Believe it or not, Wicca is one of the fastest growing religions in the world which makes total sense as those who practise 'the Craft' can take charge of their own lives and make their own choices in a natural way. There are many misconceptions about witchcraft, one being what a witch looks like. The way they have been portrayed throughout history doesn't help. Mention a witch to someone and the first thing their mind will conjure up is a hag with a large hooked nose resplendent with warts, wearing a tall pointy black hat, flying a broomstick with the obligatory black cat on the back!

The reality is that if a witch passed you in the street nowadays you probably wouldn't even notice as they are ordinary people who work, raise their families and live in ordinary houses. I haven't studied witchcraft fully but I do have a 'Book of Shadows' where I write down my thoughts and how I feel, and I have practised my own spells for some time and each of them has been successful. Whether that makes me a fully-fledged witch or not who knows? I have been called a lot worse, so bring it on!

Funnily enough, I was at a local spirit and craft fair recently doing some clairvoyant readings when a young man came over to me and asked outright, "Are you a Wiccan, or pagan?" For once in my life I was stumped for words! Once I had regained my composure, I said, "I feel I am a little bit of both", as I do believe they are a part of my spiritual make-up.

Some practising witches join modern covens but they are not for everyone – people whom I know practise the Craft prefer to study and practise in their own home environment. Being a witch is all about respecting the world by being frugal and having a good balance between material gain and spirituality. For example, being respectful of nature by caring for plants, trees and animals, and being aware of how much damage is being done to the environment. Basically, it is all about freedom of spiritual choice and taking personal responsibility for everything we do and say.

When I did my Angel Magic course I had to perform spells with an angelic theme and one of them involved invoking the 'elemental angels' who rule the elements of earth, air, fire and water. Witches also believe that all nature is made up from these elements together with a fifth element, which is spirit. All of these combined make up themselves and the world around them. If you need to know more about witchcraft you can do your own research and of course we live in the world of technology with a lot of information on the Internet about witchcraft in the Dark Ages right up to the present day and the modern witch. However, be very careful when studying this way as it would be difficult to differentiate between what is accurate and what is myth. Be aware that not everything that is written about on the Web is authentic, so use your discretion. You can't go wrong if you buy a book that has been written by a practising, experienced witch (see my Bibliography).

Z is for Zen

"It is easy to believe we are each waves and forget we are also the ocean!"

—JON J MUTH

Established 2,500 years ago, Zen is a Buddhist principle meaning 'meditation' in Japanese. The saying 'feeling Zen-like' indicates that we should live fully in the present moment. One way to explain it fully is by the Zen Master who wrote, 'Lightning flashes, sparks fly! In one blink of an eye you have missed seeing.' I could even change the last bit to, 'Life has passed you by.' Think beautiful botanical gardens, orchids in full bloom, the sound of a waterfall in a secret and peaceful location – this is Zen.

THE END

But you know by now of course that this isn't the end – it's only the beginning... And to prove the point in the nicest possible way, here is a message channelled through me by the angels, which is a message for each and every one of you:

Take time to read the words in this book and, as you do so, you will reach a new chapter in your own life. We have impregnated each page of the original manuscript with healing vibrations which you will feel as you turn the pages, and you will be able to move on in your life to new and better things. Go with our love and blessings and remember to reach out to others who are less fortunate than you. More than ever, focus on the beauty from within and you will illuminate others with your love and light.

Bibliography & Favourite Resources

Books

The Celestine Prophecy (James Redfield)

The Craft in the City – being a modern witch (Tudorbeth)

The Real Witches' Handbook – a complete guide to the Craft (Kate West)

Spirit Revelations – prophetic dreams and synchronicities (Nigel Peace)

Animal Spirit Guides (Steven D Farmer PhD)

Advanced Psychic Development (Becky Walsh)

The Crystal Bible (Judy Hall)

The Angel Bible (Hazel Raven)

The Psychics' Bible (Jane Struthers)

Conversations with the Children of Now (M Blackburn Losey)

Life Is Calling (Stephanie J King)

The Psychic Biker Meets the Extreme Ghost Hunter (P Green and S Lambert)

Websites

My own website is: *www.spiritualit.net*

For Carol Ryder's illustration and portraiture: *www.carolryder.com*

For holistic health care (spiritual and metaphysical): *www.drstandley.com*

For dreams and synchronicity: *www.spiritrevelations.com*

For life quotes and sayings: *www.quotegarden.com*

To discover the meaning of your dreams: *www.dreammoods.com*

A doorway to signs and symbolic messages: *www.whats-your-sign.com*

And for other spiritual books, of course: *www.local-legend.co.uk*

Spiritual magazines

Prediction (the UK's first MBS magazine)
Kindred Spirit
The Magical Times

The Rescue Mediums TV Show

The Rescue Mediums show is filmed in Canada, airing on W Network and OWN. It is directed and produced by Lamport & Sheppard Entertainment Ltd. The show also airs in the UK on CBS Reality and is shown in other countries around the world.

CPSIA information can be obtained
at www.ICGtesting.com
Printed in the USA
BVHW040413011221
622944BV00008B/182